Palgrave's Critical Policing Studies

In a period where police and academics benefit from coproduction in research and education, the need for a critical perspective on key challenges is pressing. Palgrave's Critical Policing Studies is a series of high quality, research-based books which examine a range of cutting-edge challenges and developments to policing and their social and political contexts. They seek to provide evidence-based case studies and high quality research, combined with critique and theory, to address fundamental challenging questions about future directions in policing.

Through a range of formats including monographs, edited collections and short form Pivots, this series provides research at a variety of lengths to suit both academics and practitioners. The series brings together new topics at the forefront of policing scholarship but is also organised around who the contemporary police are, what they do, how they go about it, and the ever-changing external environments which bear upon their work.

The series will cover topics such as: the purpose of policing and public expectations, public health approaches to policing, policing of cyber-crime, environmental policing, digital policing, social media, Artificial Intelligence and big data, accountability of complex networks of actors involved in policing, austerity, public scrutiny, technological and social changes, over-policing and marginalised groups, under-policing and corporate crime, institutional abuses, policing of climate change, ethics, workforce, education, evidence-based policing, and the pluralisation of policing.

Andy Phippen · Emma Bond

Policing Teen Sexting

Supporting Children's Rights While Applying the Law

palgrave
macmillan

Andy Phippen
Bournemouth University
Poole, UK

Emma Bond
University of Suffolk
Ipswich, UK

ISSN 2730-535X ISSN 2730-5368 (electronic)
Palgrave's Critical Policing Studies
ISBN 978-3-031-31454-4 ISBN 978-3-031-31455-1 (eBook)
https://doi.org/10.1007/978-3-031-31455-1

This Palgrave Macmillan imprint is published by the registered company Springer Nature Switzerland AG
The registered company address is: Gewerbestrasse 11, 6330 Cham, Switzerland

Contents

1	**Introduction**	1
	1.1 Overview	1
	References	5
2	**Teen Sexting: A Modern, Cultural Phenomenon? Or Not So New?**	7
	2.1 Introduction	7
	2.2 Childhood and Sexuality	9
	2.3 Researching Sexting with Young People	11
	2.4 Children's Views	16
	2.5 "But It's Illegal"	20
	2.6 Young People's Views on Police	32
	2.7 Conclusions	34
	References	35
3	**Legal Challenges**	41
	3.1 Introduction	41
	3.2 International Perspectives	44
	3.3 Geographical Challenges and the UK Position	47
	3.4 The Online Safety Bill 2023	55
	3.5 Conclusion	56
	References	57

4 **Understanding the Police Response: Putting Sticking Plasters over Legislation** 59
4.1 Introduction 59
4.2 The Application of Sticking Plasters 60
4.3 What Does This Mean for Young People? 66
4.4 Conclusions 75
References 75

5 **The Challenges of Diversionary Intervention** 77
5.1 Introduction 77
5.2 A Criminal Justice Process 79
5.3 An Analysis of Intervention at the Grass Roots 83
5.4 Facing the Policing Challenges 90
References 91

6 **A Progressive Future?** 93
6.1 Teen Sexting as an Error of Judgement 94
6.2 Headstart Kernow 96
6.3 Harm Reduction and Online Harms 99
6.4 What Works? 106
6.5 A Change in the Law 110
6.6 Conclusions 111
6.7 Personal Reflection 112
References 114

Index 115

List of Figures

Fig. 4.1	A Scatter Plot of Arrests vs Outcome 21s issued	71
Fig. 4.2	A Bubble Plot showing volume of outcome 21s (x axis), 22s (y axis) and arrests (size)	74
Fig. 6.1	An online safeguarding ecosystem	105

List of Tables

Table 4.1	Prosecutions of minors charged under section 1 of the Protection of Children Act	67
Table 4.2	Arrest and Outcome 21 recording from Home Office crime code 86/2 from 30 police forces	70
Table 4.3	Arrest, Outcome 21 and Outcome 22 recording from Home Office crime code 86/2 from 33 police forces	73

CHAPTER 1

Introduction

Abstract The digital world introduces numerous challenges to policing, such as geography, intent and the application of legislation developed in analogue times to the digital behaviours. Against a backdrop of public sector cuts and ever more scrutiny, we explore the (arguably) relatively new phenomenon of teen sexting—the exchange of intimate images via digital devices by minors—and its challenges in both supporting victims of abuse arising from the fallout of such acts, and applying the law when we know the law is not fit for purpose.

Keywords Sexting · Policing · Child protection · Children's rights

1.1 Overview

The United Kingdom, in a period of austerity, is witnessing public services, including policing, and is struggling to maintain expected levels of service delivery (Pepper et al., 2020). "Future challenges for the police and their partners working in Criminal Justice Systems include calls for service becoming increasingly complex" (Rogers et al., 2022, p. 329) and "the challenges facing contemporary policing with regards to technological developments and the impact and opportunities these

A. Phippen and E. Bond, *Policing Teen Sexting*, Palgrave's Critical Policing Studies, https://doi.org/10.1007/978-3-031-31455-1_1

provide (legitimate and illegitimate), should not be underestimated" (Manning & Agnew, 2020, p. 79). One such example is that of sexting—the exchange of intimate images via digital devices by minors. As we set out in this volume, the complexity of sexting, even though it is hardly a new phenomena, is poorly understood and prohibitive approaches underpinned by outdated and blunt legal frameworks have consistently revictimized children and young people, criminalising the very people that the law was intended to protect and, in some cases, failed to recognise the more harmful incidences of grooming, coercion and adults sexually abusing children.

This book is about the challenges faced in effectively and proportionately responding to sexting. It is about understanding *risk* and understanding *harm*. This initial chapter introduces both the topic of teen sexting and the structure of the book. It overviews the foundations of teen sexting as a modern, cultural phenomenon and explores responses from the media, policymakers and society, with a particular focus on the rhetoric around it and public dialogues.

We also draw on the more recent developments in evidence-based policing which describe policing practices guided by research evidence to demonstrate their effectiveness (Telep & Sommers, 2019). As academic researchers with many years of experience in evaluating *what works* in online safeguarding (amongst other abuse-related fields), we have borne witness to this approach gaining popularity across the public sector—nursing, public health, education, crime prevention and certainly in policing. The College of Policing has invested considerable resources in developing the evidence-based policing (EBP) agenda, Higher Education Institutions have developed educational courses and training at all levels to meet sector demands for EBP to underpin contemporary policing practice and societies, for example, the Society of Evidence-Based Policing[1] (online) have formed nationally (and globally) to connect "police officers, police staff, and research professionals who want to improve policing from within by using the best research evidence".

> Recent years have witnessed an increased emphasis on an evidence-base and 'what works' agenda in policing in the United Kingdom. This coincides with the wider policy rhetoric of the need to professionalise policing; financial cuts to policing post-2008 recession; and the changing nature of crime (such as the increase in online crimes, the threat of terrorism and

[1] See https://www.sebp.police.uk.

> the investigation of 'hidden' crimes such as historical investigations of child abuse). (Lumsden & Goode, 2018, p. 813)

Sexting, certainly appears as an example of the changing nature of crime. It is well recognised that the internet emerged as a space for children's developing sexualities and intimate relationships and their construction of a gendered, sexual self-identity (Bond, 2011). While it is often seen as a modern phenomenon across social media, we argue it has been around for a couple of decades from when we started researching children's experiences of technology in 2002. With the growth in social media and increased public and political discourse both about and on social media, there is an increased awareness that "social media is not just a place where crime and justice are discussed; it's a place where crime happens" (Salter, 2017, p. 5) as the quote below from a police officer illustrates:

> *"Sexting is a major issue here in schools and the content to do with that as I think the understanding from young people is not that good and neither is the understanding from parents as to what a sexual image might be. I think it is really important that children and young people really do understand what those images relate to, where the law stands in relation to those images as well, and what the consequences can be for those young people and for their development in the future. It is called into us on a regular basis from schools." Police officer.* (Taken from Bond & Rawlings, 2016)

As we set out in Bond and Phippen (2020) both the affordances (Hutchby, 2001) and interoperability of communication technologies, social media, artificial intelligence and the internet of things are facilitating a complex myriad of new ways to communicate, share and collaborate, transforming the landscapes of crime and giving rise to new challenges for law enforcement and everyday policing responses. In this volume we have attempted to offer a more detailed analysis than in Bond and Phippen (2020) in which we addressed the control of sexting, balancing risk against potentially heavy-handed use of the criminal law against consensual, everyday non-abusive image sharing by young people.

Methodologically we draw upon many years of experience working in schools and colleges, and with the wider children's workforce, on many different facets of online harms. We will reflect upon already published historical work, and whether policy developments have changed outcomes for young people. Somewhat typically we will present some perspectives from what has become, through the years, an ethnography of practice around teen sexting. In presenting novel empirical work, we will apply both quantitative and qualitative methods to look at both the national perspective (breadth) and practitioner experiences (depth) to draw conclusions on current policing practices upon children and young people related to the exchange and further non-consensual distribution of intimate images.

Chapter 2 considers the wider debates on sexuality and childhood, earlier research in relation to sexting and different stakeholder views. We argue that the dominance of adultist agendas and outdated legislation have revictimised children and indeed criminalised them rather than actually protecting them while children's own views have been silenced. Furthermore, we are mindful that Chapter 2 is a little repetitive and talks about various pieces of empirical work resulting in the same outcomes. This is deliberate. If you find it repetitive reading it, imagine conducting this research over the last fifteen years and discovering the same outcomes which clearly evidences nothing is changing for young people!

Chapter 3 continues by outlining key legal challenges in the UK, the out-of-date legislation and prohibitive mindsets which are contrasted with grassroots explorations of youth behaviours and presents the difficulties faced by contemporary police practice in enforcing the law, public interest, supporting vulnerable minors and maintaining public consent. Within this context, we introduce the Outcome 21 and 22 processes, which have evolved, arguably to allow police to maintain the application of legislation clearly out of date while being mindful of the challenges that present, and the impact upon young people.

With the broad topic established, this remainder of the volume provides the reader with insights into the methods used (both quantitative and qualitative including the broadly ethnographic) and the theoretical and conceptual underpinnings of the discourses examined in relation to teen sexting. Chapter 4 provides a quantitative analysis that focusses on a nationwide exploration of how both the legislation has been applied to enter young people into the criminal justice system, and the application of both Outcome 21 and 22 on cases involving the youth distribution of intimate images, which paints a picture of inconsistent practice and the fabled "postcode lottery".

Chapter 5 develops the empirical exploration of contemporary policing around teen sexting to explore in more detail how both Outcome 21 and 22 are applied through dialogue with youth justice professionals. Again, our data highlights the frustration of practitioners and the inconsistency of application, often with the best of intentions, as a result of a dearth of national coordination and consistency of process advice. This, conversely, highlights how trying to address poor legislation with superficial fixes will often complicate matters further. Finally, Chapter 6 draws these discussions to an end, with a reflection upon the repetitive nature of our work in this area over the years and how the cycle might be broken, by considering more progressive approaches within the restrictive criminal justice imposed upon those who work in child protection.

References

Bond, E. (2011). The mobile phone = bike shed? Children, sex and mobile phones. *New Media & Society, 13*(4), 587–604.

Bond, E., & Phippen, A. (2020). Tackling teen sexting-policing challenges when society and technology outpace legislation. In H. Jahankhani, B. Akhgar, P. Cochrane, & M. Dastbaz (Eds.), *Policing in the era of AI and smart societies* (pp. 157–177). Springer.

Bond, E., & Rawlings, V. (2016). *Multi-agency E-safety Crime Prevention project report.* University of Suffolk. https://www.uos.ac.uk/sites/default/files/EBMESCP-Final-Report-Dec2016v2.pdf. Accessed January 2022. Published as Bond, E., & Rawlings, V. (2017). Virtual vulnerability—Safeguarding children in digital environments. In M. Dastbaz, H. Arabnia, & B. Aghkar (Eds.), *Technology and smart futures.* Springer.

Hutchby, I. (2001). Technologies, texts and affordances. *Sociology, 35*(2), 441–456.

Lumsden, K., & Goode, J. (2018). Policing research and the rise of the 'evidence-base': Police officer and staff understandings of research, its implementation and 'what works.' *Sociology, 52*(4), 813–829. https://doi.org/10.1177/0038038516664684

Manning, M., & Agnew, S. (2020). *Policing in the era of AI and smart societies* (H. Jahankhani, B. Akhgar, P. Cochrane, & M. Dastbaz, Eds., pp. 59–82). Springer. ISBN 978303050613.

Pepper, I., Rogers, C., & Martin, H. (2020). Evidence based policing: A view on its development within the police service. *Journal of Work-Applied Management, 12*(1), 91–96. https://doi.org/10.1108/JWAM-01-2020-0001

Rogers, C., Pepper, I., & Skilling, L. (2022). Evidence-based policing for crime prevention in England and Wales: Perception and use by new police recruits. *Crime Prevention and Community Safety, 24*, 328–341. https://doi.org/10.1057/s41300-022-00158-w

Salter, M. (2017). *Crime, justice and social media.* Routledge.

Telep, C. W., & Somers, L. J. (2019). Examining police officer definitions of evidence-based policing: Are we speaking the same language? *Policing and Society, 29*(2), 171–187. https://doi.org/10.1080/10439463.2017.1373775

CHAPTER 2

Teen Sexting: A Modern, Cultural Phenomenon? Or Not So New?

Abstract While there are some who might view teen sexting as a modern, digital phenomenon, and therefore a new challenge to policing and legislation, we argue that while the act might be modern, the motivations centre around young people and sexual agency, risk and risk mitigation. We review consistent patterns in research findings over almost twenty years to highlight that prohibitive approaches and "just say no" messages are doomed to fail. Over this period, while the focus has been on wrongdoing and eliminating the act of intimate image exchange, policymakers and safeguarding professionals have failed to listen to the youth voice, their needs and their rights.

Keywords Teen sexting · Children's rights · Moral panic · Risk · Youth voice · Online harms

2.1 Introduction

This first chapter proper overviews the previous literature around teen sexting and the wider cultural context around this phenomenon. In doing so it begins with an exploration of the body of knowledge, differentiating between the repetitive (measuring prevalence and motivations) with

A. Phippen and E. Bond, *Policing Teen Sexting*, Palgrave's Critical Policing Studies,
https://doi.org/10.1007/978-3-031-31455-1_2

the progressive (representing the youth voice and rights-based perspectives) and the social construction of childhood, youth, risk and sexuality. Understanding the social construction of risk is central to our arguments presented throughout this volume and questions about risks and hazards feature increasingly in public discourse (Culpitt, 1999). It is well established that risk anxiety is central to the social construction of contemporary childhood (see for example, Scott et al., 1998) and we have argued for many years that "it is the notion of vulnerability that shapes the nature and the consequences of adult concerns and behaviours towards children in late-modern society" (Bond, 2014, p. 27).

> mostly associated with adolescents, sexting, broadly speaking, refers to the production of and sharing of a naked or semi-naked image or a sexualized message via digital technology. Understanding sexting behaviors, however, is rather more complex and current commonly used definitions do not adequately address the different types of sexting and the different motivations and consequences that sexting behaviors have. Both media and public discourse have centered on the risks of sexting in relation to children and young people, as have policy responses to sexting activity. Concerns over a child being groomed online and being coerced or threatened into sending a naked or semi-naked picture by someone seeking sexual gratification has been the focus of policy debate and many public educational campaigns across the globe. Similarly, other campaigns have depicted the child or young person as a victim who sends a sexualized image to a peer that is then posted on a social media site or shared widely among a peer group causing the sender humiliation and distress. While these are both clear examples of digital abuse that have been the center of public awareness campaigns, it is often argued that current legal frameworks are insufficient to provide an adequate and appropriate response in many sexting cases, as there is considerable diversity in the circumstances and the contexts of sexting behaviors. As such it is argued that the (il)legality of sexting is such that it fails to recognize young people's agency and that they may be choosing to produce and share images of themselves by choice. (Bond, 2016)

Concerns over the law as it currently stands also include the fact that in relation to intimate image sharing, legislation in the UK provides protection to those aged eighteen or over in the Revenge Porn Law introduced in the UK in 2015 but those aged seventeen or under still face the threat of prosecution or the discomfort of investigation including phone forensics. While both categories face inconsistent responses from police

(Bond & Tyrrell, 2021), for those under 18 those inconsistencies can result in a criminal record (Phippen & Bond, 2020).

Sexting a clear example of a moral panic (see Cohen, 1972) provides a rationale for the cultural and policy responses and the evolution of public discourses around teen sexting as evidenced by the extensive research we have undertaken and our work with practitioners over the last twenty years. It is well acknowledged that young people establish "complex emotional and sexual relationships with peers" (Teitler, 2002, p. 151) yet policymakers and many adult stakeholders view teen sexting as something we need to stamp out yet evidence demonstrates prohibitive approaches to social issues are doomed to fail. Viewing childhood as a social construction is important in understanding how children and young people are constructed as both risky and "at risk" through the dominant discourse of innocence and evil; the child is simultaneously constructed as both victim and threat. While childhood is constructed as a time of innocence, vulnerability and dependence (Jenks, 1996), risk anxiety, engendered by the desire to keep children safe, frequently has negative consequences for children themselves and curtails their activities in ways which may restrict their autonomy and their opportunities to develop the necessary skills to cope with the world (Scott et al., 1998). Our research findings both compliment other literature in the field, and also highlight the challenges in policing this modern phenomenon, particularly given the application of current legislation which, as we will explore throughout this book, was never intended to be applied to the context in which young people find themselves growing up in. We also interrogate the legislative field around which teen sexting is policed in practice and examine in detail other regulatory instruments (see Chapter 3) in building our case to argue for a far more progressive, youth-centric "solution" to these issues in Chapter 6.

2.2 Childhood and Sexuality

Analyses of the debates on social change, the media and sexuality suggest that a liberational discourse dominates everyday and media representations of sexuality (Jackson & Scott, 2004). The affordances (Hutchby, 2001) of social media enable propinquity (nearness) and "play an increasingly important yet ubiquitous role in young people's romantic relationships in late modernity" (Bond, 2014, p. 112). The debate surrounding childhood, sexuality and media is fraught with contradictions and anxieties associated with protecting children's sexual innocence (Jackson &

Scott, 2004) and few commentators see the increased sexualisation of the media as a positive development for children (Buckingham & Bragg, 2004). To this end, cultural and social constructions of childhood are fundamental to understanding the contemporary debate on sexuality in childhood and examining the paradox between what Jackson and Scott (2004) depict as "public openness" (associated with postmodernity) and "private unease".

The impression of a sexually freer, more diverse society is reflected in representations of sexuality and intimate relations in popular culture and reinforced by the everyday knowledge gained from living in a social environment increasingly saturated with sexual imagery (Jackson & Scott, 2004, p. 234). There is a preoccupation with sexual values, practices and identities and a proliferation of sexual texts in contemporary society (Attwood, 2006). The prominence of sex and sexuality in contemporary western culture illustrates how pervasive both are and how easily sexuality encroaches into areas previously considered non-sexual (Cover, 2003). The iconography of pornography is increasingly common (McNair, 1996) and "post-modern culture arguably has enabled taboos to be transgressed through pleasing erotic imagery packaged as fashion not pornography" (Kent, 2005, p. 430). However, as Jackson and Scott (2004) point out, changes in societal attitudes simply cannot capture the complex and context-specific aspects of everyday thought and practice.

While "sex and its associations with 'new' and 'novel' inventions and technology is nothing new", the relationship between sex and technology is fundamental to understanding complex everyday lives (Barber, 2004, p. 142). We have been researching teen sexting since around 2002. During this time, we have conducted numerous surveys, spoken to thousands of young people about the issues they face around the exchange of intimate images, and what they wish for in terms of support from adults with caring responsibilities and wider society, and we have also spoken widely with stakeholders at all levels across the children's workforce. Frith (2000) argued that people are not generally comfortable talking about sex, but as Plummer (1995, p. 172) points out "people tell sexual stories to assemble a sense of self and self-identity". It should be noted here that the young people in our research over the years have volunteered the information, often unprompted by the researchers, and in fact on many occasions stated that they welcomed the opportunity to talk about their experiences and discussed the role of digital technology in sexual relationships and the sexual nature of material shared amongst themselves.

Plummer (1995, p. 16) draws on a sociological framework derived from symbolic interactionist theory to advocate sexual stories, which have been seen as routes to understanding culture in anthropology, to argue that they are "socially produced in social context". Therefore, as we argue throughout this analysis, it is understanding the *context* that is vitally important in responding to sexting behaviours, not just the specific individualised context of the actual sexting incident(s) but also the wider societal, legal and global (for example, children's rights) context.

2.3 Researching Sexting with Young People

The following details our journey in understanding the sexting phenomenon through research in the exchange of indecent images among minors, and surrounding behaviours since 2002. During that time, we surveyed over 2000 young people, in two major projects (2009 and 2017 which will be drawn out in the discussions below) and, as positivistic approaches do not address people's subjective experiences (Grover, 2004), we have undertaken qualitative research through interviews and focus groups with hundreds of young people (see for example, Bond, 2010, 2011, 2014; Bond & Rawlings, 2017). Additionally, we have facilitated discussions in assemblies, classrooms, workshops and Safer Internet Day[1] activities to explore issues around attitudes towards intimate image exchange by minors. These discussions were generally wide ranging—we did not simply say "what does everyone think about sexting?", but instead explored many different aspects such as prevalence, knowledge of legislation (and from whom was this knowledge impacted), education (if any) and the support they receive from adults.

Early work in this area arose working with an online safe charity—the South West Grid for Learning.[2] The aim was to determine the prevalence of "sexting" among Key Stage 4 (14–16) young people and its motivation that arose from discussions we (as academics and also the charity themselves) had been having with schools and colleges around sexting practices. This early research came about from visiting schools when they would disclose dealing with an incident of intimate image exchange and, in some cases further distribution, yet school leaders generally felt they

[1] See https://www.saferinternetday.org/. Accessed January 2023.

[2] See http://www.swgfl.org.uk/. Accessed January 2023.

were left to resolve the incidents with little support or national guidance. Yet, at the time when policymakers were pressed on providing support, they were generally of the view this must be anecdotal and clearly very few incidents occurred. The need for training was further evidenced by a national survey[3] we undertook in 2013 with another charity The Marie Collins Foundation which found that 70% of the respondents from Health, Education and Children's Services stated that they had not received training in online risk assessment and 96% said they would value such training and that 81% of the respondents said they had received no training in assisting children in their recovery from online abuse and 94% stated that they would value such training.

It is interesting to note that while there was resistance to accept that sexting was a common practice among young people, there remains to this day an obsession by some adult stakeholders—policymakers and press in particular—with exactly "how many young people do this?" as if by some arbitrary measurement it will be possible to see a sudden cessation of these practices despite the fact that educational approaches and the law have not changed. We also discovered from a very early time that the educational focus on the law in this area meant that developing accurate tools to measure prevalence was both practically and ethically challenging. The development of child-centred participatory research methods, influenced by the social studies of childhood (James et al., 2010) and children's rights (Alderson, 2008; Kellet, 2005) has changed the landscape of researching with children, but given that the core educational message is "don't do it, its illegal", it is very unlikely there will be an honest response from young people when asked "do you send nudes?". There is also an ethical issue arising from asking children to disclose if they have "self-generated" an image, given that, by the letter of the law, this is illegal. Therefore, while we can state with confidence, through many conversations with young people, that knowledge of the exchange of intimate images by minors is something they are very certainly exposed to, to be able to give a policymaker a statistic like "35% of young people do this" is both impossible and, we would suggest, also facile. Surely the focus of legal and policy response should not be triggered by a threshold of prevalence? It should, instead, acknowledge this modern cultural phenomenon

[3] See https://www.mariecollinsfoundation.org.uk/news/the-childrens-workforce-across-england-is-ill-equipped-to-meet-the-needs-of-child-victims-of-online-abuse. Accessed January 2023.

that has the potential to cause significant harm to young people and provide educational and legislative responses mindful of this.

As a result of the problematic nature of survey work around teen sexting, our research focus has always been on how young people view and experience the culture of intimate image exchange by minors. We tend to explore young people's perspectives to be exposed to this material, whether they are affected by it, and what their thoughts are about both those who generate material and those who share/spread it in a broader context (Bond, 2010, 2011, 2014).

Building on from this qualitative research, the early survey work in Phippen (2009), which ultimately resulted in data collected from just over 1000 14–16-year-olds, asked about awareness of images, and attitudes around these images, as a means to measure how many young people are affected by "sexting". In this preliminary work we were mindful that this was a very new area and young people might be confused or shocked by what was being asked. There was certainly nothing in the curriculum in 2009 which meant there was any need to deliver education around this topic and we had certainly been told by some senior leaders that they do not talk about it because this might encourage such behaviours! We have never seen any evidence that this was actually the case and again here return to the reluctance to deliver education around this issue being influenced more by professional's discomfort to discuss these issues and to fall back on the adage "don't do it, it's illegal".

While participant centred research has gained considerable popularity in recent years and rightly so, it was certainly far less common practice when we started this work. Our initial, and indeed subsequent work, was heavily influenced by the social studies of childhood (see for example James & James, 2004, 2008; James et al., 2010) and as such, prior to commencing the first survey, we discussed the idea with a school council (aged between 14 and 16) with whom we worked to help shape the questions in a young person friendly manner but also, more importantly, to see whether they thought it would be a worthwhile thing to do. So, in 2008, we sat down with eight young people and said (paraphrased):

Us: "We'd like to survey young people about their views on teen sexting"
YP: "What's that?"
Us: "It's when someone sends an intimate image to someone else, and perhaps the image get shared further"
YP: "Oh yeah, that happens all the time here. Why did you call it sexting?"

From this one comment, we knew the survey was timely and the research was justified. We were keen to explore attitudes and some measure of awareness, without asking specific questions about actions by the respondent. While policymakers might have been reluctant to see this as a widespread issue:

- 40% of respondents said they were aware of peers who had sent or received intimate images
- 39% said that they were aware of "one or two incidents"
- 7% said it happened regularly and 13% said that it happened all of the time
- In asking whether these images were shared beyond the intended recipient, 56% of respondents said they were aware of this happening at least once.

However, in one of the most interesting and surprising findings, which has been reflected in subsequent surveys we have conducted, when asked whether they thought that sharing further was done to upset the sender, only 22% said they thought this was the case. Hasinoff (2013, p. 2) points out "a teenager who chooses to send sexually explicit images to a peer is engaging in a very different activity than someone who distributes a private image with malicious intent or coerces another person to produce an explicit image". Which does raise the question of what do they think the intentions of someone to non-consensually share an indecent image of a peer would be? So even almost years ago we had a population of teenagers who were exposed to the "risks" around sexting, whether this is being exposed to unsolicited images, having images shared with them, or seeing the impact of the sharing of image of their peers. And given the disclosures from many respondents, many we would conclude had been exposed to what was, in the eyes of the law, illegal content.

Perhaps one of the most interesting pieces of data collection for this original survey was an open-ended question at the end asking for them to comment further on the nature of the survey and the topic we were asking about. Already, in these responses, we could observe young people expressing concerns around the tension between protection and legislation. Comments such as (paraphrased):

- "Young people need someone to talk to if this happens to them"
- "We need more education on this topic, particularly in younger years when this sort of thing starts"
- "Younger children should be told about the legalities of this sort of thing"
- "I know people who have been victim of this and they need support from adults".

There were also poignant comments about the difference between a consensual and non-consensual exchange:

- "If people shared to third parties then there should be arrested"
- "Young people should only share with a trusted partner and they need to be aware they can be shared further".

And one comment went into significant detail about the use of images to coerce further, particularly when they felt they could not ask for help for fear of being judged or told off.

Given the year of publication of this book (2023), the survey data collected fifteen years ago, and the discourse of young people then was still far more nuanced and mature than much of the recent policy discussions around this topic in the present day. As a result of "sexting" being a recurring discussion topic with both young people and staff at schools we worked with, we decided that we needed to spend a focused amount of time talking about these issues. Motivated by a piece of research by Ringrose et al. (2012), which explored legitimised sexual harassment in schools and colleges, which was exploratory and discursive in nature and resulted in significant discussions around the use of images in coercion and control, we embarked on a qualitative programme of research (including Bond, 2014; Bond & Rawlings, 2017; Phippen, 2012) that centred around focus groups with young people specifically exploring their attitudes towards these issues and how it impacts upon their lives. Around 100 young people were spoken which allowed a detailed exploration of what was emerging from the many assemblies, classes and workshops we were carrying out. There were a number of key findings that were drawn from this work that again highlighted how the culture of self-generation was impacting this generation.

2.4 Children's Views

Giddens' (1992) notion of the transformation of intimacy that emotional communication replaces traditional ties in late modernity and that sexual love and relationships are transformed. Sexting is a clear example of how intimacy has been transformed in late modernity with technology overcoming traditional geographic and physical boundaries in relationships.

> The recognition of children's social agency and active participants in research has significantly changed children's position within the human and social sciences and led to a weakening of taken-for-granted assumptions found in more conventional approaches to child research. In order to hear the voices of children in the representations of their own lives it is important to employ research practices such as reflexivity and dialogue. (Christensen, 2004, p. 165)

Our analysis of both our own body of research to date and the wider field of sexting research (see for example among others Albury, 2016; Albury & Crawford, 2012; Hasinoff, 2013, 2015; Ringrose et al., 2012; Setty, 2019, 2020a, 2020b) illustrates how technology, including social media, are simultaneously viewed as both supportive but also potentially damaging, thus exemplifying the double-edged sword of modernity discussed by Giddens (1990) and Ling's (2004) assertion that the mobile phone is associated with both constructive and potentially harmful implications. This paradox is often illustrated in young people's conversations which frequently highlight both the positive and negative aspects of social media in their relationships. Their construction of their sexual selves in intimate relationships are portrayed and illustrated within group dynamics and their discussions they often actively constructed their identity within the group through current and previous relationships including sexual experiences (Bond, 2010, 2014; Phippen, 2012; Setty, 2019, 2020a, 2020b).

There is a blurring of the boundaries between the public and the private. What could be perceived as being private—the naked body or the sexual act—is transformed into being public by technology. It is then shared (usually consensually within the context of an intimate relationship) and then made more public to a wider audience (non-consensually) and consequently being perceived in terms of risk. Exemplified by the quotes (taken from fieldwork undertaken in 2006 and published in Bond, 2014) the first of which depicts Megan's discussion of a girl who had sent intimate pictures of herself to her boyfriend (private). However, when the context of the relationship changed, the images had been shared (public) and the public/private boundaries blurred:

> Megan [aged 17]: *"A girl was taking pictures of herself, revealing pictures shall I say? And sent them to her boyfriend – they like split up and he sent them to like everyone and everyone found out who it was and that and everyone knew so".*

In another example Tilly, John and Sid discuss a boy masturbating in front of a webcam; the images were sent to girls that he knew at school. The girls had saved the images to their mobile phones and had subsequently shared the images to others at school.

> Sid [aged 16]: *"Oh yeah he has web cam on and he was wanking over the web cam".*
> Tilly [aged 16]: *"Oh yeah to these girls and they saved it on their phone and sent to everyone".*

In another focus group, girls discussed their experiences of viewing sexual content produced by boys known to them:

> Laura [aged 14]: *"Yeah like the boys flashing like their meat and two veg".*
> Pip [aged 14]: *"Yeah and they are like 'show us your blah blah blah'".*
> Laura [aged 14]: *"Yeah and they are like oh! Oh! Mine are better than his – do you know what I mean? And it's just like competition".*

Tilly (aged 16) in her discussion of using technologies and mobile phones in everyday life, described how a friend of hers had been sent sexual images, by someone that she did not know. Tilly's account also highlights how technology can make it difficult to control the risk, as you cannot see what the image is before you open it. She viewed this occurrence as becoming more common with advances in technologies and that it was not easy to prevent this from happening:

> Tilly [aged 16]: *"Yeah and weird stuff. Like well you know [laughter] ... you know like that does happen and like with girls at school as well with the new 3G video calls".*
> Sid [aged 16]: *"Did she not know who it was?"*
> Tilly [aged 16]: *"She only saw his penis!"*
> Sid [aged 16]: *"She didn't recognize it then?"*

Tilly [aged 16]: *No! I should hope not – like apparently he was like talking to someone on a 3G chat site and they arranged to like call each other like you know … doing stuff and then her number had come up instead of the other girl's.*
Tilly [aged 16]: *"He called her by accident – yeah – having a wank".*

Jackson and Scott (2004, p. 243) argue that sexual activity occurs behind closed doors but that the "merging of boundaries associated with sexual intimacy produces fragility and renders us vulnerable to loss of self-confidence, self- esteem and indeed a loss of self when relationships end" and the fear associated with the thought that "intimate knowledge has escaped the confines of the relationship" and is being shared with others.

The concept of *risk* in childhood during the twentieth century has been dominated by developmental and welfare models of childhood (Hood et al., 1996) which fail to acknowledge that children. However, many of the young people who have talked to us over the years, viewed themselves as being responsible for keeping themselves safe and notions of responsibility were an important part of their construction of self-identity. They weighed up the perceived risks in their individualised situations and circumstances and responded with certain behaviours in order to manage the potential risks. This is a clear example of Qvortrup's (2005) observation that the relationship between social change and constructions of childhood is often seen through the conceptual lens framed by "structure" and "agency".

Childhood sociology, emphasising children's positions as social actors, as creative and inventive users of the world around them, has nurtured conceptual and empirical explorations of children's competency and agency (O'Brien et al., 2000). While there have been significant changes in how children are viewed in some fields of research and children's rights have been acknowledged and arguably championed in some aspects of policy, one of the fundamental findings from our analysis is that the wishes of young people have not changed, as we will explore below. Therefore, we would argue that the current approaches to "supporting" young people in this area have failed. "Utopian and dystopian approaches can be understood as substantive or determinist theories of technology, since they postulate that the architecture of the internet and social media necessarily generates specific kinds of identities, practices, relationships and societies" (Salter, 2017, p. 19). This is arguably because much online safeguarding policy has adopted a utopian approach, focused on an unrealistic aim to *eradicate* harmful online behaviours, rather than adopting a realistic evidence-based approach, which recognises, understands and aims to *mitigate* their impact.

Risk is, as we have previously argued, central to understanding responses to sexting. Consideration of Beck's (1992) Risk Society thesis provides a helpful insight into a theoretical explanation of risk which we revisit in Chapter 6 to suggest a more effective response to sexting for the future. Risk is defined as:

> A systematic way of dealing with the hazards and insecurities induced and introduced by modernisation itself. Risks as opposed to older dangers, are consequences which relate to the threatening force of modernisation and tom its globalisation of doubt. (Beck, 1992, p. 21)

Risk and risk management strategies have profound implications for self-identity, as through risk profiling and adopting risk-taking behaviours, children achieve identity as individuals and as members of cultural groups (Green, 1997). It is also important to consider the difference between risk and harm when examining approaches to online abuse. Salter (2017, p. 7) defines "online abuse" as "the misuse of social media and other online communication platforms with the intent to cause harm or offence to another person or persons". We have consistently argued that a key challenge in effectively supporting young people who might become victims of abuse because of non-consensually sharing intimate images, is that adultist perspectives have dominated:

> *Young people are taking intimate images of themselves and sharing them with others. We want to put an end to this.*

As we outline above children's intimate, sexual relationships are viewed as risky in adult discourses (Bond, 2014). Of course, we fully acknowledge the risks associated with young people sharing intimate images with peers and the potential harm that arises because of further coercion, non-consensual further sharing and uncontrolled distribution. However, we know, given the prevalence of teen sexting within the schools and colleges with whom we work, that the prohibitive messaging as a risk management strategy has failed and is certainly not protecting young people from harm.

2.5 "But It's Illegal"

The prevalent "educational tool" that is used in schools and colleges, often with invited talks by police officers, is based on the rather strange view that "if we tell them it's illegal, they won't do it". A standard practice, in many schools, seems to be an annual school assembly whereby a police officer delivers a scary talk about the harms that can result from sharing images (with standard tropes like ending up in paedophile archives and child arrests for the distribution of "child pornography") which is clearly intended to frighten young the audience, rather than inform them. We will, therefore, in the final chapter, draw heavily on parallels between such educational approaches for online harms and the drug prevention educational strategies of the 1980s and 1990s, another such prohibitive approach which resolutely failed to achieve its intended goals of preventing young people from taking illegal drugs with similar messaging of "don't do it, because its illegal". Furthermore, in the case of teen sexting, this ineffective approach is reinforced in the current school curriculum. In England and Wales, the national curriculum for Relationships and Sex Education (UK Government, 2021), the only reference to exchanging intimate images in the entire document is in the section entitled *The Law*, which states (page 30):

> *82. It is important to know what the law says about sex, relationships and young people, as well as broader safeguarding issues. This includes a range of important facts and the rules regarding sharing personal information, pictures, videos and other material using technology. This will help young people to know what is right and wrong in law, but it can also provide a good foundation of knowledge for deeper discussion about all types of relationships. There are also many different legal provisions whose purpose is to protect young people and which ensure young people take responsibility for their actions.*

Even within this single paragraph, there is much troubling rhetoric—ensuring young people know what is right and wrong in law, without any further discussion around in problematic application of law—in the case of teen sexting—in scenarios that were never envisioned when the legislation was developed. And, perhaps most concerning, knowing about the law means young people can take responsibility, which seems at odds with other discussions around youth responsibly, for example, Gillick competence (Children's Legal Centre, 1985) (explored further in subsequent chapters). If the only message for education professionals around teen sexting, in the statutory documentation for the delivery of relationships and sex education, is that young people are responsible for their actions should they break the law, how can this possibly effectively support young people in understanding the issues, mitigating risk, or knowing where they might get help and advice?

Jenks (2005) helpfully develops Foucault's idea of spatial control to argue that the manipulation of space is a primary example of adults controlling children's worlds and this postmodern diffusion of authority has not led to democracy but to experiences of powerlessness, not as a potential source of identity but as a prescription for victimisation. A recent training workshop with some pastoral tutors at a college with whom we work provides an illustrative example of the problematic nature of this attitude of "but it's against the law so they should not do it". During a discussion on the sharing of intimate images by young people, it was pointed out that while the law states that the taker of the image is breaking the law, the criminal justice process is not set up so that it would be highly unlikely that they would be charged, and the message simply shuts down routes for disclosure for young people. The following is a paraphrasing of the conversation that followed:

> Pastoral tutor: *"But it is illegal"*
> Trainer: *"Yes, but it is also acknowledged by the criminal justice system that it is not in the public interest to prosecute a minor in most cases"*
> Pastoral tutor: *"If it's illegal they need to be told"*
> Trainer: *"Even if it will do nothing to help the young person?"*
> Pastoral tutor: *"If it's illegal they shouldn't be doing it"*
> Trainer: "*But we know the law is being applied in ways in which it was not intended. Police, judiciary and CPS all acknowledge this"*
> Pastoral tutor: *"If they're breaking the law they shouldn't be doing it"*
> Trainer: *"But they are"*

And so on....

While there are many different views on this across the children's workforce, and many police officers with whom we have spoken (see Chapters 4 and 5) are clear they do not view it as a good use of their time to scare vulnerable children who are victims of abuse as a result of exchanging images. However, there are many who still hold views similar to those in the illustration above. In another recent discussion with a safeguarding lead in a school, when asked how they support a young person who discloses the non-consensual sharing of intimate images, their response was "First, we give them the hairdryer treatment, then we generally call the police". Thus, given the failings of this approach, and while we do not doubt that the majority of those who work with and support children are doing so because they wish to help them, we do question why this approach remains so prevalent. And the answer appears to be that it is because it is easier to tell a child not to do it and make use of the law to scare them, rather than trying to understand the nuances and context around the acts of exchanging images and the relative impact based upon these factors to effectively provide advice and support.

Yet, the last thing a vulnerable teenager whose images are being shared around their peers needs to hear is either:

Haven't you been stupid?

Or

You've broken the law, you're in trouble now!

As Renold's (2005) analysis of children's sexual and gender relationships emphasises, children are simultaneously "sexual beings" and also "sexual becomings" and adults tend to fear and avoid recognising children's sexuality and seeing them as sexual beings. We know from our research that the impact of these educational messages on young people is severely detrimental. It results in young people unwilling to disclose or, if they do disclose, not receiving any support in ameliorating the issues they are facing. A simple random sample of disclosures from Everyone's Invited, a website where child victims of sexual harassment and abuse in schools anonymously disclosed their experiences,[4] highlights many cases of young people talking about these prohibitive messages and lack of support.

- A young person who had intimate images shared non-consensually at the age of 13, who still suffers anxiety issues at the age of 21 as a result. The victim states that she blames herself.
- A young person pressured into sending nudes at the age of 12, who did so because she thought "that's how dating is these days".

[4] Everyone's Invited Website. https://www.everyonesinvited.uk. Accessed January 2023.

- A young person who, after a sexual encounter with a peer, with the peer then claiming he'd taken images non-consensually and shared them with his friends. When she was sent the images, they were not of her, but when she disclosed the abuse to a teacher, instead of support they received a lecture on the dangers and legalities of sharing nudes.

These disclosures reflect the conversations we have had with young people and what we have heard from educational practitioners including a recent example of a 16-year-old female student consensually sharing imitate images of herself with her male student partner (also 16) whom subsequently shared them non-consensually with their wider peer group. When the incident was discovered by the school, the response was to expel the female student and the male student received no punishment. We have asked young people, on many occasions over the years, to whom they would disclose to if someone had non-consensually shared images of them, and most said there was no way they would speak to a teacher or parent. Far better, and less "risky", from their perspectives was to talk it through with their peers.

The adultist position of teen sexting the centres on the act of image exchange and sexuality and childhood. Sexting refers to the exchange of the image between the taker and receiver and this *gifting* (see Berkling, 1999; Maus, 2002) has become an important part of children's everyday friendships and relationships (Bond, 2014). However, seemingly, as a society, we do not want minors taking indecent images of themselves and sending them to others. Given the prevalence of digital technology and ease of distribution, is this utopian goal a realistic one? By maintaining our gaze on the act of the gift, rather than exploring motivations and the broader context in which the act occurred—for example, was it consensual, were there elements of coercion, was there consent for sharing, does the young person appreciate the nature of coercion, either as perpetrator or victim?

To draw on the often-quoted US researcher dana boyd (2011): "teen sexting is a very rational act with very irrational consequences".

It is a very sensible summary of the act itself and the potential fallout. Given everyone feels, to some degree, that attractiveness is a highly desirable quality, and being in a relationship is an important part of knowing you are attractive, and with the means by which to take "selfies" and send them easily, why wouldn't they engage in these practices? Yet the irrationality of the consequences can be significant—rapid and uncontrolled redistribution, posting online, seen by thousands—is something new to this phenomenon. It is this part of the act that differs from generational similarities for the desire to be in a relationship, or to be told one is attractive. It is complicated.

As we have argued above, even the term "sexting" is something of a media creation at odds with the behaviours young people engage with and observe in their peers. A key observation from many conversations with young people is that the term "sexting" is rarely used by young people. Generally speaking, they refer to "nudes" and "dick pics" (Setty, 2020a). The distinction between the two is clear for young people. And while the term sexting is applied equally in the eyes of adults should the image be requested or unsolicited this is not the view of young people. For example, dick pics, where some boys will view the unsolicited sharing (gifting—see Berkling, 1999; Maus, 2002) of a photograph of their genitals as part of a "courtship ritual"—a means to establish a relationship with the recipient. While this might, generationally, seem peculiar in the extreme for those who did not grow up in an age when the taking and distribution of intimate images was not so straightforward, given how poorly these issues are covered in the curriculum, might they be forgiven for assuming this is part of the twenty-first-century courtship ritual? For nudes, our work over the years has highlighted that it is clear girls are far less likely to volunteer images like this, however, they may send "nudes" as part of a relationship, or in response to requests (sometimes repeated and persistent) from a boy (see also Setty, 2019, 2020a, 2020b). Our emphasis on the importance of understanding context underpins our arguments throughout this book in relation to the legislation and how it *can* and *should* be applied. These two, admittedly simplified, but very different scenarios would fall into a "sexting" incident where the same justice process might be applied. Clearly there are a multitude of various different examples we can draw on and all have complex patterns of structure, agency (Giddens, 1979) and coercion (see Stark, 2007). But, in the eyes of the law and the justice system in the UK, it is important to remember that all acts involving intimate images of a person under the age of 18 are illegal.

We also would like to point out that terms such as "youth produced indecent images" are also unhelpful in that they imply a voluntary engagement with the production and distribution of the image and do little to shift adultist views from victim blaming and prohibition rather than supporting young people and their rights. Similar to the definition in the PSHE curriculum, this terminology implies that the young person who took the image, as a law breaker, needs to accept what happens as a result. The context is ignored and the act takes precedence.

> Children's safety in connected media is vital, but it needs to be understood in the contact of the spectrum of their digital rights, for example, in balance with children's rights of provision and participation in the convention on the Rights of the Child. Agency is as crucial to positive, effective use of digital media as safety is. Without the agency needed to participate and exercise rights, children can neither take advantage of the opportunities digital media afford nor develop resiliency when facing risks. They must be encouraged to think critically and develop their own language, views, strategies, associations and interests as users on connected digital media. (Third et al., 2014, p. 8)

We have argued for many years that the centring of the youth voice is essential in this arena. We would urge any professionals supporting young people experiencing the impact of intimate image exchange to first listen to them and not to judge. Adult bias has come to dominate many aspects of professional practice and sadly there are many adults, practitioners and academics alike, who believe they know what young people are doing, and have the solution to ensuring young people do not engage in these practices. That approach, as outlined above, is one of prohibition—do not do it, it is illegal. However, they rarely actually listen to what young people have to say which has as best negative and at worst harmful consequences for young people. It does not prevent young people from exchanging images, but siloes and silences impacts their mental health and can result in further abuse that could have been prevented. A consistent response over many years of our empirical work when asking young people what are the best things adults can do to help them in the event of harm or abuse arising from the sharing of images, is that they want to be listened to and not judged. This has been a constant in our research for many, many years. And sadly we are consistently told that adults have let them down.

The legislation is clear—anyone taking an indecent image of a child (defined in law to be anyone under the age of 18) is breaking the law, regardless of whether they have that image in their possession, or they distribute it further. Therefore, anyone "self-generating" an indecent image of themselves under 18 is breaking this law, regardless of whether they forward the image to others. Furthermore, anyone receiving the image will be breaking the law, regardless of whether they forward the image to others.

Advice by the UK's National Society for the Prevention of Cruelty to Children (NSPCC) on sexting carries similar warning[5]:

The law says that creating or sharing sexual images or videos of a child under 18 is illegal, even if the person sharing is a child. This includes:

- *sending sexual messages to a child*
- *a child taking an explicit photo or video of themselves or a friend*
- *sharing an explicit image or video of a child, even if it's shared between children of the same age*
- *having, downloading or storing an explicit image or video of a child, even if the child gave their permission for it to be taken*
- *sharing an explicit image or video of a child is illegal, even if it's shared between children of the same age*
- *'Sharenting' - or adults sharing a photo of a child to raise awareness is also illegal.*

Although it is caveated with the somewhat imprecise:

Whilst it's illegal for anyone to exchange nude or semi-nude imagery of a child, the legislation is there to protect children from abuse. If an incident involving a young person sharing a nude is reported to the police, it is very unlikely it will result in the child being prosecuted.

Again, this information is incomplete and ambiguous in its language and provides little reassurance to a minor who has, for example, been coerced into producing an indecent image of themself and sending it to their abuser and is subsequently scared to tell anyone because they have been told that what they have done is illegal. Therefore, we suggest that this is not a pragmatic application of legislation ensuring children are protected from abuse.

"Young people's use of social media is giving shape and form to intimate coercion and sexual harassment. This effect is particularly acute for

[5] NSPCC. (n.d.). *Sexting*. https://www.nspcc.org.uk/keeping-children-safe/online-safety/sexting-sending-nudes/.

girls and young women, who are at disproportionate risk of humiliation and intimidation through online invasion of privacy" (Salter, 2017, p. 17). Again, this highlighted the importance of youth-centric and case-by-case response, rather than assemblies about legalities and threats of prosecution. We are mindful of the diversity of sexting practices across relationships and sexualities, and in drawing on the experiences of the young people who volunteered their views, there was general agreement that boys were far more likely to "volunteer" an image to a girl (discussions in relation to heterosexual relationships were more frequent in the qualitative data) and girls were more likely to self-generate as a result of a request, either voluntarily or through pressure from their peers (see also Hasinoff, 2013). However, pressure to share was not necessarily viewed by the young people as coercion but as a means that someone wanted to get an image of someone. There was general agreement from the young people that harm and abuse will generally arise as a result of the non-consensual sharing to third parties, rather than the initial production and sharing of the image. As it is worth noting from Setty's (2020a, p. 574) qualitative study with young people suggests that "risk and shame discourses affect the social landscape for young men, as well as young women".

What was also clear from those early datasets was that the young people had not received any meaningful education around intimate image exchange or how they might disclose in the event of abuse arising as a result of sharing. Sex education at the time (and arguably still does) generally centred around biological reproduction (or "how not to get pregnant") and the spreading of Sexually Transmitted Infections (STIs). Unsurprisingly coverage of "sexting" was generally delivered in assemblies as prohibitive, rather than educative. The closest any young people came to discussing self-generation practices was being told that it was illegal. Alongside other simple messages the like of which we have grown both familiar with and weary of over the years—things such as "once its online, it's always online" or "you can't control it once you've pressed send". Two messages which, while patently untrue, also result in young people concluding that if this is the case, there is no point is disclosing or asking to get support and the abuse that might result from the sharing of the images is the logical consequence of their actions and they deserve it. There was no acknowledgement from any education received that something can be done in the event of an image being shared, or that this is something that, sadly, is something tackled by schools on a daily basis across the country. Prohibition, it seemed, was the core of what meagre "education" the young people did receive around sexting. Thankfully with educational resources like "So You Got Naked Online",[6] information for young people is finally improving.

As a result of this lack of empathy and knowledge by adult stakeholders, it is unsurprising that most young people believed that such issues should be dealt with at a peer level, preferably not involving adults and the advice they would give peers was to work through the upset because shame is transient. In a few weeks, someone else would be the focus of ridicule and abuse, therefore it is best left to die down on its own. Many viewed the inclusion of adults in any resolution as a guarantee of making things worse and being blamed themselves.

While our research and professional/practical reputation grew, and we becoming known as the "go to" individuals for speaking with young people, police and other professionals about sexting, it was apparent that attitudes towards victims of abuse and where the blame lay had changed very little. This was though, in our experience, one aspect of a culture of victim blaming or slut shaming (Ringrose et al., 2013) which is not limited to digital spaces. One of the most concerning areas of "sexting" we observe from working with young people is the problem of "victim blaming"—someone sends an image, the recipient shares that image, the victim then receives abuse from the wider community because they are a "slut" or a "slag" for sending the image to this one trusted individual (Phippen, 2016). There is very focus on challenging the behaviour of the individual who spread the image further, just the person who took the image. In the earliest survey conducted, almost 75% of respondents said the person responsible for the image is the person who took it, even though in many instances that image might have been generated through peer pressure, harassment or coercion. Such victim blaming attitudes are not limited to young people but are more likely to be attached to females. For example, we were told by one school when we were asked to provide some workshops for young people that they had invited the local constabulary in a few weeks before to talk to the students about keeping safe as part of a countywide "Safer Streets". The police officers who had visited the school and spoken in an assembly had focused on female students not "wearing short skirts and low-cut tops" when going

[6] See https://swgfl.org.uk/resources/so-you-got-naked-online/. Accessed January 2023.

out for the evening because it could "send out the wrong message" and not getting drunk as they "may make bad decisions". A survey undertaken by Bond and Tyrrell (2021) found that the police in the United Kingdom have a limited understanding of revenge pornography legislation and lack confidence both in investigating cases and in effectively responding to victims. A more public example[7] accused police of hanging "victim blaming" baubles on a Christmas tree in a church. "Don't drink to excess" and "being drunk makes you vulnerable" are printed messages serving as decorations for Suffolk Constabulary's festive tree, according to images posted on social media.

Subsequent surveys included questions in 2017 around motivations. While we were unsurprised by prevalence, we were aware through conversations with young people that the act of exchanging images occurred in a wide range of scenarios with different motivations. When asked about motivation 67% thought people sent nudes because they wanted a relationship, 68% to be told they were attractive, and 66% because they were pressured into doing it. We also saw the influence of the prohibitive approach to education very clearly. 64% of respondents agree to some level with the statement "Sending nudes is illegal and people shouldn't do it". Interestingly, more felt those who spread images further are subject to illegality, with 83% agreeing with the statement "Spreading a nude is to other people is illegal and people shouldn't do it".

Crucially, once again, when asked about the role adults with responsibility for child welfare have in these scenarios, when asked what they can do most to help, 72% of young people said they wanted "safe spaces" to be able to get advice without the threat of punishment (harking back to a comment made by a respondent in 2009). 74% said "don't judge", 76% said "listen", and 70% said "have open and honest conversations". Almost ten years on from the original survey work, young people were asking the same things, and still not getting support.

Further discussion around legislation in the focus groups highlighted this further—young people have consistently been told self-generation among minors is illegal, however, they are not sure why, what laws the legality relates to, or the broader legal context around it. As we will explore in detail in Chapter 3, the law, if explored in depth, is clearly

[7] See https://www.independent.co.uk/news/uk/home-news/christmas-tree-victim-blaming-baubles-drunk-assault-suffolk-police-ipswich-a9228221.html. Accessed January 2023.

a mess and has been subject to many legal sticking plasters to compensate for the fundamental flaw in applying legislation to a practice never envisaged. To explain the illegality arising from a 1978 law, updated in 2003, written in a time where self-generation was never envisaged, and then cross referenced with CPS advice that says most prosecution of minors would fail the public interest test, and then compounded with "no further action" crime outcomes which may or may not come back to haunt the individual in the future is complex. However, this was appreciated far more by young people than "don't send nudes, its illegal". One girl said that they had experienced an assembly a couple of years earlier when a member of the police came in and, in her words, "scared us to death" about the trouble they could get in if they took nudes, saying that the message being delivered by a member of law enforcement made it even more frightening. This did not, she said, mean her peers stopped doing it. It just made them more scared to disclose in the event of an image being shared further.

An interesting case (interesting because blame, and prosecution in this case was apportioned to the sharers of the images, not the original taker) we often used with young people is a 2015 (Metro, 2015) prosecution of two teenaged boys for the possession and indecent images of a minor (although reported in the media as "revenge pornography"). One of the boys was in a relationship with a girl of similar age and during that time she had sent him as many as 170 images. When their relationship ended she asked for the images to be destroyed. However, it came to light that the boy (14 at the time) had sent two images to his friend (then 15) in exchange for £10. When the girl was made aware of this, she alerted the police and the boys were arrested. They were both found guilty and sentenced to 12-month referral orders and were made to pay costs. In this case, we would reflect on a pragmatic application of the law—the victim was not charged, and the motivation, being financial, was a mitigating factor in demonstrating awareness by those distributing the images for profit and it seems reasonable that they were charged and found guilty.

However, from an educational perspective it is an interesting case because of the blame lying at the feet of the sharer and recipient, rather than the victim. Social media commentary at the time still suggested a focus on her. For example, a comment from a poster on social media in response to a local newspaper reporting the story suggested that the victim was at fault for sending the images in the first place and that she had ruined the abuser's life by doing so. This, we would suggest, is no surprise if the educational message is given centre entirely on legality and facing up to "responsibilities" without exploring the more complex issues around pressure and coercion. If young people aren't even aware of consent or coercion as concepts, how are they going to understand that consent is contextual? One cannot telegraph one image share to another, in the same way that consent to sexual intercourse with an individual does not immediately extend consent to all future situations.

Even with the advent of revenge pornography law in 2015 which clearly states that the non-consensual sharing of an image is illegal, therefore offering protection to the victim, safeguarding is not communicated effectively to young people. If a victim, who is suffering abuse, harassment, bullying or exploitation as a result of self-generating an image believes that it is their fault that they are suffering harm because the image is their responsibility in the eyes of the law, we are failing to protect children from the potential serious harm that arises from these behaviours.

It is interesting the reflect upon the fact that some areas of safeguarding have become more progressive. For example, if two minors engaging in consensual sexual activity, it would be extremely unlikely that if a pregnancy had arisen as a result, those with safeguarding responsibility's first response was to tell them they had broken the law and could be subject to prosecution. It is highly likely in a school setting, as long as competence to consent is established, the first safeguarding response will be one of support and sexual health. However, it seems that the digital nature of the exchange of nudes means this pragmatism is lost by the professional. Perhaps, given that this would not be something the professional experienced in their formative years, they cannot empathise in the same way they might with an "offline" sexual experience.

One other message we often hear from safeguarding professionals (teachers, advisors, police) which we might argue is another form of absolution of responsibility on their part, is that sexting among teens is now "normal"—it's something "they are all doing" and we should therefore not worry about it. Or, to put it another way, it's not something I wish to get involved with and it's their own fault if they end up being abused or emotionally harmed as a result.

There is certainly a tension between freedom of expression and safeguarding for young people—there are indeed provisions within the Data Protection Act 2018 (UK Government, 2018) (s4.1.a) that specifically mention modification to privacy rights in the event of:

The processing is necessary for the purposes of—

(i) *protecting an individual from neglect or physical, mental or emotional harm, or*
(ii) *protecting the physical, mental or emotional well-being of an individual,*

Therefore, it should never be the view of anyone with safeguarding responsibilities that this is simply not something to worry about. Again, we refer to the context of the exchange of images, rather than the actual act of exchange. Any disclosure around intimate image abuse requires some level of investigation to determine whether coercion, control or abuse formed part of the motivation for the production or exchange of images. Indeed, the case above where the young man sold images of his ex-girlfriend shows the importance of providing legal protection for victims. However, our concerns lie in the fact that the victim of the abuse, if the law is applied accurately and correctly is at risk of criminalisation as well as the abuser. And what we are exploring in this book is how challenging policing become when this challenge is presented, where difficulties in the law are acknowledged, yet those in power are unwilling to change the law, therefore police and the wider criminal justice system have to apply imprecise workarounds instead.

In bringing these attitudes and views up to date, and completing our empirical observations around the attitudes of both children and the children's workforce, we will return to our experiences with the Headstart Kernow project, a children's mental health project in the South West county of Cornwall in the UK in Chapter 6 (explored in far more detail in Phippen & Street, 2022a, 2022b). The project's main goal was developing tools for early intervention with children's mental health concerns across the children's workforce based upon Bronfenbrenner's ecology of child development (Bronfenbrenner, 1979), a model that has influenced our own thinking about approaches of online risk and safeguarding that we will explore later in this volume.

2.6 Young People's Views on Police

Finally in a book that considers the challenges of policing this social phenomenon, we should also reflect here on the perceptions of the police by young people, particularly related to our discussions with them. In our original survey on sexting in 2009, we asked which adults young people would turn to for support. The largest response to this question (70%) was that they would speak to friends instead. However, police would be turned to by 25% of respondents (slightly higher than the lowest category—Teachers, at 21%). While we did not ask this question in further surveys, we have discussed the role of police in safeguarding around sexting with young people over the course of the last fifteen years and views seem to have changed very little in this time.

As we can see from the statistic above, young people, it seems, would be very unlikely to turn to the police should they be harmed, or at risk of harm, as a result of the exchange of intimate images. Discussion with young people about this presents little surprise. Police, in the views of young people, have two roles in these scenarios:

- The *educator* who comes to the school in uniform and in an assembly tells them that engaging in these practices is illegal and if you get caught you could end up ruining your future career and also risk arrest
- The *enforcer* who is called to the school as a result of a peer disclosing harm as a result of a sexting incident, whose role is punitive in nature, ranging from a good telling off to arrest.

The educator role is one we recognise from many discussions with young people, and also school staff. A default position by a lot of safeguarding leads in schools with whom we have spoken is that sexting is an issue best tackled with a talk from a local community liaison or support officer because the prohibitive message they wish to be delivered is better coming from someone with legal authority. The assemblies are, as one might expect, generally brief and harsh in tone, with clear messages about not sending intimate images without any nuance on the reality of the criminal justice context and public interest. We have certainly never heard of a school visit that took a nuanced view and urged anyone who might be being harassed or coerced as a result of engaging in image exchange to speak to the police because they can help. And, given the expectations of the national curriculum around teen sexting, as discussed above, this is not a surprise. Why go beyond the demands of the curriculum? However, the impact of these, as we have shown with the samples from the Everyone's Invited website, can be lasting and long term. As one young woman told us in an anecdote about a police assembly around sexting, the impact for her was to be terrified of either engaging in, or receiving, an image, because of the long-term impact on their lives. However, when asked whether they felt the assembly would prevent peers from doing just that, she said she was doubtful.

Regarding the enforcer role, to be fair to policing professionals, when challenged on the view that arrest might occur, young people generally will not know of an immediate peer who has been arrested. However, there are always rumours of someone "at another school" or similar being arrested for this. And we have certainly heard about cases where young people knew of incidents in school where police had been called and the victim of abuse had been subject to "investigation" in front of school staff and parents (including, in some cases, examining of their phone for further images), which generally resulted not in resolution for the victim, but further upset.

Police are not viewed as a stakeholder who might support, and when asked about whether they thought police would have their best interests in mind, and help to resolve the abuse or harms, most young people did not recognise this role. Hardly a surprise, we would suggest, giving the main exposure they have to police related to sexting is the prohibitive assembly.

2.7 Conclusions

In this chapter we have explored our own empirical work and that of others considering attitudes towards teen sexting by both young people and also stakeholders in their safeguarding. As we have shown, we have been working in this area for a long time and after almost a generation, young people's needs and professional's responses are virtually unchanged. Jenks (2005) developed Foucault's ideas of spatial control to suggest that the exercise and manipulation of space is a primary example of adults controlling children's worlds and suggests that the postmodern diffusion of authority which far from leading to democracy but to an experience of powerlessness and a prescription for victimisation leaving children figuring only as symbolic representations of this welter of uncertainty, both literally and metaphorically. In reality, young people understand there are risks associated with exchanging images, including legal ones, but some will still engage in such practices. Professionals generally bring a fairly one-dimensional view that what they are doing is illegal, therefore they should not do it. This is similar in nature to a lot of the historical approaches around drugs harms, until recently. These parallels will be explored in far more detail later in this book. However, in drawing this chapter to a close we would conclude that, given this extensive empirical work, young people are correct, in general, not to disclose to those professionals who should be in a position to help and support them. Which, surely, is the antithesis of good safeguarding practice. Put simply, adults continue to let young people down in this area, because, it seems, it is far easier to deliver a basic prohibitive message than to consider and investigate a disclosure on its merits to determine the content around the act of image exchange, rather than focussing upon the act of image exchange and its legality (applying legislation that never considered the producer of the image might be both subject and distributor of the image, and could also be a minor).

However, we are not without sympathies for professionals tackling these issues and, in theory, supporting young people at risk of harm. This is particularly relevant to police, who, given a disclosure of law breaking are duty bound to investigate and apply the law. The law, which we will explore in far more detail in the next chapter, is clearly not fit for purpose. This has resulted in the justice system applying work arounds and imprecise "solutions" in order to acknowledge the legalities of the act, while also attempting to better reflect the best interests of the child. However, these practices are not without unintended risks and outcomes for young people, as we will explore in more detail in Chapters 4 and 5.

References

Albury, K. (2016). Sexting, schools and surveillance: Mediated sexuality in the classroom. In G. Brown & K. Kath Browne (Eds.), *The Routledge research companion to geographies of sex and sexualities* (pp. 359–367). Taylor and Francis.

Albury, K., & Crawford, K. (2012). Sexting, consent and young people's ethics: Beyond Megan's Story. *Continuum, 26*(3), 463–473. https://doi.org/10.1080/10304312.2012.665840

Alderson, P. (2008). *Young children's rights: Exploring beliefs, principles and practice* (2nd ed.). Jessica Kingsley Publishers.

Attwood, F. (2006). Sexed up: Theorizing the sexualization of culture. *Sexualities, 9*(1), 77–94.

Barber, T. (2004). Deviation as a key to innovation: Understanding a culture of the future. *Foresight, 6*(3), 141–152.

Beck, U. (1992). *Risk society: Towards a new modernity*. Sage.
Berkling, H. (1999). *The sociology of gifting*. Sage.
Bond, E. (2010). Managing mobile relationships—Children's perceptions of the impact of the mobile phone on relationships in their everyday lives. *Childhood, 17*(4), 514–529.
Bond, E. (2011). The mobile phone = bike shed? Children, sex and mobile phone. *New Media & Society, 13*(4), 587–604.
Bond, E. (2014). *Childhood, mobile technologies and everyday experiences*. Palgrave.
Bond, E. (2016). Sexting. In M. Brown & N. Rafter (Eds.), *Oxford research encyclopaedia of crime, media and popular culture*. https://doi.org/10.1093/acrefore/9780190264079.013.142
Bond, E., & Rawlings, V. (2017). Virtual vulnerability—Safeguarding children in digital environments. In M. Dastbaz, H. Arabnia, & B. Aghkar (Eds.), *Technology and smart futures*. Springer.
Bond, E., & Tyrrell, K. (2021). Understanding revenge pornography: A national survey of police officers and staff in England and Wales. *Journal of Interpersonal Violence, 36*(5–6), 2166–2181. https://doi.org/10.1177/0886260518760011
boyd, d. (2011, June 13). *Teen sexting and its impact on the tech industry*. Read Write Web 2WAY Conference, New York, NY.
Bronfenbrenner, U. (1979). *The ecology of human development*. Harvard University Press.
Buckingham, D., & Bragg, S. (2004). *Young people, sex and the media: The facts of life?* Palgrave Macmillan.
Children's Legal Centre. (1985). Landmark decision for children's rights. *Childright, 22*, 11–18. Gillick v West Norfolk & Wisbech Area Health Authority, UKHL 7.
Christensen, P. H. (2004). Children's participation in ethnographic research: Issues of power and representation. *Children and Society, 18*(2), 165–176.
Cohen, S. (1972). *Folk devils and moral panics*. MacGibbon and Kee.
Cover, R. (2003). The naked subject: Nudity, context and sexualization in contemporary culture. *Body & Society, 9*(3), 53–72. https://doi.org/10.1177/1357034X030093004
Culpitt, I. (1999). *Social policy and risk*. Sage.
Frith, H. (2000). Focusing on sex: Using focus groups in sex research. *Sexualities, 3*(3), 275–297.
Giddens, A. (1979). Agency, structure. In *Central problems in social theory contemporary social theory*. Palgrave. https://doi.org/10.1007/978-1-349-16161-4_3
Giddens, A. (1990). *The consequences of modernity*. Polity Press.

Giddens, A. (1992). *The transformation of intimacy: Sexuality, love and eroticism in modern societies*. Polity Press.

Green, J. (1997). Risk and the social construction of social identity: Children's talk about accidents. *Sociology of Health and Illness, 19*(4), 457–479.

Grover, S. (2004). Why don't' they listen to us? On giving power and voice top children participating in social research. *Childhood, 11*(1), 81–93.

Hasinoff, A. A. (2013). Sexting as media production: Rethinking social media and sexuality. *New Media & Society, 15*(4), 449–465. https://doi.org/10.1177/1461444812459171

Hasinoff, A. A. (2015). *Sexting panic: Rethinking criminalization, privacy, and consent*. University of Illinois Press.

Hood, S., Kelley, P., Mayall, B., Oakley, A., & Morrell, R. (1996). *Children, parents and risk*. Social Science Research Unit.

Hutchby, I. (2001). Technologies, texts and affordances. *Sociology, 35*(2), 441–456.

Jackson, S., & Scott, S. (2004). Sexual antinomies in late modernity. *Sexualities, 7*(2), 233–284.

James, A., & James, A. (2004). *Constructing childhood: Theory, policy and social practice*. Palgrave Macmillan.

James, A., & James, A. (2008). *Key concepts in childhood studies*. Sage.

James, A., Jenks, C., & Prout, A. (2010). *Theorizing childhood*. Polity Press.

Jenks, C. (1996). *Childhood*. Routledge.

Jenks, C. (2005). *Childhood* (2nd ed.). Routledge.

Kellet, M. (2005). *How to develop young children as researchers*. Paul Chapman Publishing.

Kent, T. (2005). Ethical perspectives on the erotic in retailing. *Qualitative Market Research: An International Journal, 8*(4), 430–439.

Ling, R. (2004). *The mobile connection: The cell phone's impact on society*. Morgan Kaufmann.

Maus, M. (2002). *The gift*. Routledge.

Metro (2015). Youngest person to be convicted for 'revenge porn' sold ex-girlfriend's photos on Facebook for £10. https://metro.co.uk/2015/02/02/youngest-person-to-be-convicted-for-revenge-porn-sold-ex-girlfriends-photos-onfacebook-for-10-5046135/ [Accessed May 2023]

McNair, B. (1996). *Mediated sex: Pornography and postmodern culture*. Arnold.

O'Brien, J., Jones, D., & Sloan, D. (2000). Children's independent spatial mobility in the urban public realm. *Childhood, 7*(3), 257–277.

Phippen, A. (2009). *Sharing personal images and videos among young people*. South West Grid for Learning & University of Plymouth.

Phippen, A. (2012). *Sexting: An exploration of practices, attitudes and influences.* https://library.nspcc.org.uk/HeritageScripts/Hapi.dll/filetransfer/2012SextingExplorationPracticesAttitudesInfluencesReport.pdf. Accessed January 2023.

Phippen, A. (2016). *Children's online behaviour and safety: Policy and rights challenges.* Springer.

Phippen, A., & Bond, E. (2020). *Organisational responses to social media storms: An applied analysis of modern challenges.* Springer.

Phippen, A., & Street, L. (2022a). *Online resilience and wellbeing in young people.* Palgrave Macmillan.

Phippen, A., & Street, L. (2022b). *Digital resilience tool.* https://www.headstartkernow.org.uk/Digital/Headstart%20online%20resilience%20tool%20WebV2.pdf. Accessed December 2022.

Plummer, K. (1995). *Telling sexual stories: Power, change, and social worlds.* Routledge.

Qvortrup, J. (2005). *Studies in modern childhood: Society, agency, culture.* Palgrave.

Renold, E. (2005). *Girls, boys and junior sexualities: Exploring children's gender and sexual relations in the primary classroom.* Routledge.

Ringrose, J., Gill, R., Livingstone, S., & Harvey, L. (2012). *A qualitative study of children, young people and "sexting": A report prepared for the NSPCC.* National Society for the Prevention of Cruelty to Children.

Ringrose, J., Harvey, L., Gill, R., & Livingstone, S. (2013). Teen girls, sexual double standards and 'sexting': Gendered value in digital image exchange. *Feminist Theory, 14*(3), 305–323.

Scott, S., Jackson, S., & Backett-Milburn, K. (1998). Swings and roundabouts: Risk anxiety and the everyday worlds of children. *Sociology, 32*, 689–705.

Setty, E. (2019). Meanings of bodily and sexual expression in youth sexting culture: Young women's negotiation of gendered risks and harms. *Sex Roles, 80*, 586–606. https://doi.org/10.1007/s11199-018-0957-x

Setty, E. (2020a). 'Confident' and 'hot' or 'desperate' and 'cowardly'? Meanings of young men's sexting practices in youth sexting culture. *Journal of Youth Studies, 23*(5), 561–577. https://doi.org/10.1080/13676261.2019.1635681

Setty, E. (2020b). *Risk and harm in youth sexting: Young people's perspectives.* Routledge.

Slater, M. (2017). *Crime, justice and social media.* Routledge.

Stark, E. (2007). *Coercive control: How men entrap women in personal life.* Oxford University Press.

Teitler, J. O. (2002). Trends in youth sexual initiation and fertility in developed countries: 1960–1995. *Annals of the American Academy of Political and Social Science, 580*, 134–152.

Third, A., Bellerose, D., Dawkins, U., Kelties, E., & Pihl, K. (2014). *Children's rights in the digital age; A Download from children around the world*. Young and Well Cooperative Research Centre. https://www.unicef.org/turkiye/en/reports/childrens-rights-digital-age-download-children-around-world

UK Government. (2018). *Data Protection Act 2018*. https://www.legislation.gov.uk/ukpga/2018/12/contents. Accessed December 2022.

UK Government. (2021). *Relationships and sex education (RSE) and health education*. https://www.gov.uk/government/publications/relationships-education-relationships-and-sex-education-rse-and-health-education. Accessed January 2023.

CHAPTER 3

Legal Challenges

Abstract One of the fundamental challenges in policing teen sexting lies in the efficacy of legislation developed for one purpose now being applied to another. While the focus of this study lies in the legal and social contexts within England, because this is where we conduct the majority of our research, there are similar legislative approaches in other jurisdictions. If we explore the development of these laws, we can see that, while that are debated with the best of intentions, unintended consequences, such as the application of law designed to protect children from exploitation being applied to those victims, can result.

Keywords Legislation · Teen sexting · Protection of Children Act 1978 · Online Safety Bill 2023 · Safeguarding

3.1 Introduction

This chapter explores legal responses to teen sexting. The focus is on legislation in England and Wales, the foundation of which is Section 1 of the Protection of Children Act (PCA) 1978 (UK Government 1978) and comparable legislation such as The Civic Government (Scotland) Act

A. Phippen and E. Bond, *Policing Teen Sexting*, Palgrave's Critical Policing Studies, https://doi.org/10.1007/978-3-031-31455-1_3

1982 (UK Government, 1982). Exploration of the inception of this legislation, and its subsequent application in debate, will highlight the flaws in applying this legislation in ways that were not envisaged during its introduction in 1978 and 1982, respectively. It will continue by intersecting the legislation with the advent of teen sexting, and its initial application, policy responses and public discourse, contrasting both the support and criticism of the policing of this “crime”. Agency responses to the issues arising from the criminalisation of children as a result of police action are explored, particularly Crown Prosecution Service and College of Policing Guidance, and the chapter discusses in detail the evolution of Outcome 21 and 22 and responses by police when considering youth offending around teen sexting. We contrast this with legislation and support for adult victims of image-based abuse under the Revenge Porn Law form 2015 compared to the punitive nature of the policing responses to teen victims and highlight the challenges of policing in acknowledging the legal flaws.

While the previous chapter was very much centred on youth voice and introduced some of the challenges of applying the law in a prohibitive manner to social behaviours not ever considered at the time of the law’s introduction, this chapter will consider the legislation in more detail, while always being mindful of the youth voice in this analysis. However, prior to the introduction of the legal discussion, we should also consider the influence of children’s rights within the context of teen sexting, and the impact of the legalisation on these rights. While we have touched briefly upon these rights, when considering safeguarding provisions in the Data Protection Act, there are more issues to consider when determining the efficacy or, indeed, the morality of applying these laws in the manner to which they are now, in some cases, applied.

A fundamental starting place for any consideration of children’s rights is the UN Convention on the Rights of the Child (United Nations, 1989), ratified and accepted by the UK in 1989. Therefore, one would anticipate, this would be writ large in any legislation that claims to be in the best interests of the child. However, as we have discussed in the previous chapter, the prohibitive use of the law, from both enforcement and education, results not in the best interests (Article 3), but actually has a negative impact upon a child’s rights. If we consider, as a starting point, the consensual exchange of intimate images between two teenagers in a relationship, where there is no risk of harm or abuse that arises from the exchange, we immediately see conflict if we are to apply the letter of the law. Should the law be applied as a result of the discovery of this exchange, we immediately see a conflict with the further rights. Firstly, Article 12 (respect for the views of the child) is immediately in conflict. While the child does not wish for any legal intervention, in the event of disclosure and investigation by police officer, this should be the anticipated outcome. Furthermore, the perennial (in child online safety scenarios) Article 16 (the right to privacy) immediately comes into conflict.

What is interesting in all the years that we have been working and researching in this field there is little evidence of a rights-based approach to education. This is in spite of the fact that the convention states that children need to know and understand their rights and the rights of others and that schools should provide children's rights education but that many children remain in the dark about their rights and as such schools are failing children (Covell et al., 2017). The production and sharing of images, in a consensual and non-harmful manner could, we would argue, form part of the legitimate exploration of sexual identity and a way to express themselves in a sexual manner (see Bond, 2011). Therefore, we might also suggest that Article 13 (freedom of expression) rights are also impacted by a prohibitive approach to educational and legal responses to the sharing of images. Children certainly should expect, in any society that is respectful of their rights, that their sexual development and expression should form part of their rights to privacy and, regardless of provisions for safeguarding we have already discussed as part of the Data Protection Act 2018, should be protected. While there are certainly safeguarding exemptions, we would question the safeguarding concerns around the exchange of intimate images between two consenting fifteen year olds. While the legal arguments may appeal to certain adult stakeholders who do not wish minors to have a sexual identity or private life, that does not mean they should develop prohibitive messages without full knowledge of the law and children's rights.

Furthermore, should the incident of exchange result in the non-consensual further sharing of images, additional rights might also be breached as a result of legal intervention applying the UK legislation. If we take, for example, a case of a fifteen-year-old sharing, consensually, intimate images with their partner. In the event of the relationship breaking down, the partner then chooses to share the images further. If the subject of those images is mindful that, as a result of the education they have received, should disclose to an adult that this sharing has occurred, they risk arrest and subsequent investigation because they "should not have taken the images in the first place", they are unlikely to disclose. As such, the victim is increasingly vulnerable, as a result of what they have been told by adults with safeguarding responsibilities, to sexual coercion or exploitation and abuse from peers. As such, both Article 19 (protection from violence, abuse and neglect) and Article 34 (sexual exploitation) may both come under attack. And we should be mindful that these erosions of rights have come directly from adults who are supposed to have their best interests at heart.

In contrast, should the fifteen year old do similar three years later they would be protected from the non-consensual sharing of the images, rather than being fearful of arrest. With the introduction of what are sometimes clumsily referred to as "revenge porn" laws, which arose as a result of concerns about the rise of image-based abuse among adults, the partner subject to prosecution[1] under Section 33 of the Criminal Justice and Courts Act 2015, updated in the Domestic Abuse Act 2021 (UK Government, 2021) to consider even the threat to share being an arrestable offence. While the law is still by no means perfect, it offers considerably more protections for adults than minors, whom we might consider deserving of more protection.

```
A person commits an offence if—
(a) the person discloses, or threatens to disclose, a private
sexual photograph or film in which another individual ("the
relevant individual") appears,
(b) by so doing, the person intends to cause distress to that
individual, and
(c) the disclosure is, or would be, made without the consent of
that individual.
```

3.2 International Perspectives

As we have discussed in the introduction, the focus of the legal analysis in this book lies in the UK, with a particular focus on the Protection of Children Act 1978 (ibid.). However, we should also stress that the legislation in the UK differs very little from other jurisdictions, many of

[1] Albeit within the challenges of the legislation around "revenge pornography" such as proof of intention to abuse (see Phippen & Brennan, 2020).

which equally apply laws around child pornography to the exchange of intimate images between minors.

Drawing on recent discourse on the use of terminology,[2] we emphasise that we purposefully do not use the term "child pornography" in this context. The term when applied to the behaviour and victimisation of minors is problematic in itself. There has been much discussion in the last few years over the use of the term "pornography" applied to children (for example Kettleborough, 2015) and Interpol's definitions.[3] The term "pornography" implies consensual sexual acts between two, or more, parties. However, as defined in law, a child cannot consent to sexual acts and are not willing participants. Nevertheless, this is still a term that is used in much legal discourse around the world, which is why we will refer to it in this context in this brief exploration.

In Australia, where a federal system allows both commonwealth and state laws, division 473.1 of the Commonwealth Criminal Code (Australian Government, 1995) defines child pornography as any sexual image of a minor, and the code also defines crimes to "access, transmit or make child pornography" (section 474.19) and to "possess or produce child pornography with the intent to place it on the Internet" (sections 474.20, 474.23). However, as can be seen from the citation, this legislation was established at the very start of the Internet age and as explored in Lee et al. (2015), while the law is in place, it is difficult to determine when it is applied in minor-on-minor offences and there is certainly no attempt to differentiate between cases where the subject and taker of the image are the same, and they are a minor. Nevertheless, there has been little political appetite to amend the law to ensure minors cannot be found guilty of the manufacture and distribution of child pornography in peer-oriented cases.

In 2010, when this issue was debated, the then Minister for Home Affairs, Brenan O'Connor (2010) stated:

> *Excluding the sending of child pornography or child abuse material by young people from the proposed offences would be inappropriate, as it might reduce protections for young people. For example, instances of young people sending*

[2] See https://www.iwf.org.uk/about-us/our-campaigns/no-such-thing/. Accessed January 2023.

[3] See https://www.interpol.int/en/Crimes/Crimes-against-children/Appropriate-terminology. Accessed January 2023.

> *sexually explicit images of themselves or other young people may in some cases be malicious or exploitative. Although the child pornography offences could potentially apply to young people, there is scope for law enforcement and prosecution agencies to take the circumstances of a particular case into account before proceeding to investigate or proceeding to prosecute.* (2010, p. 2052)

Similar tensions lie in the US, where efforts to police teen sexting are equally enmeshed with child pornography legislation, as explored in detail in Sacco et al. (2010) and Sweeny (2013). In Canada, the same legal debates are explored in Slane (2013), which states:

> *Section 163.1 of the Criminal Code of Canada defines child pornography as including any visual representation (photographic or drawn) that shows a person who is under 18 (or depicted as under 18) engaged in explicit sexual activity, or which depicts the sexual organs or anal region of a person under 18 for a sexual purpose. The definition also includes written material that advocates or counsels sexual activity with a person under 18, or which describe illegal sexual activity with a person under 18.*

There is, however, a caveat in Canadian law:

> *It is an offence to make, distribute or possess such materials, unless the materials are serving a legitimate purpose that does not cause undue harm to minors*

Although, clearly, the legitimacy of minors exchanging images would still be debatable.

And we can see familiar challenges across the EU (Crofts & Lievens, 2018) where there is still a strong link between child pornography protections under Directive 2011/93/EU (European Parliament, 2011) and its application to teen sexting. However, it is interesting to note in this directive there is specific guidance for member states to apply discretion should possession or distribution be applied to minors in non-coercive scenarios:

> *It shall be within the discretion of Member States to decide whether paragraphs 2 and 6 of this Article apply to cases where it is established that pornographic material as referred to in Article 2(c)(iv) is produced and possessed by the producer solely for his or her private use in so far as no pornographic material as referred to in Article 2(c)(i), (ii) or (iii) has been used for the purpose of its production and provided that the act involves no risk of dissemination of the material.*

However, this makes mention of private use (i.e. self-production) rather than focus on the age of the taker/distributor (who might very well also be the subject). Nevertheless, it would seem that few member states have implemented this exemption. It is certainly not the case in the UK, and post-Brexit would seem even less likely. This brief review of the typical approach to policing teen sexting, and its enmeshing with child pornography protections, are certainly at the heart of UK legislation. The legislation that is applied to teen sexting in the UK, the Protection of Children Act 1978 (ibid.), was introduced as a private members bill with the best of intentions by Cyril Townsend MP.

3.3 Geographical Challenges and the UK Position

The foundation of the legislation makes it illegal for someone to generate and distribute an indecent image of a child. It is without question that in the event of self-production and voluntary sharing of an intimate image of themselves, the victim will also be the perpetrator under this legislation. However, as we have already highlighted, the legislation was introduced and debated at a time before the day when someone might have the technical capability to produce an image of themselves in a private setting and make use of a global communication network to distribute it to a consenting recipient. In the era where the legislation was established, the means to produce and distribute such imagery was costly and time-consuming, and would be virtually impossible for the subject of the image to be the taker and distributor of the image.

From a punitive perspective, within the legislation teen sexting is unambiguously illegal under s1 PCA:

it is an offence for a person—

(a) *to take, or permit to be taken [or to make], any indecent photograph [or pseudo-photograph] of a child...; or*
(b) *to distribute or show such indecent photographs [or pseudo-photographs]; or*
(c) *to have in his possession such indecent photographs [or pseudo-photographs], with a view to their being distributed or shown by himself or others; or*

(d) *to publish or cause to be published any advertisement likely to be understood as conveying that the advertiser distributes or shows such indecent photographs [F4or pseudo-photographs], or intends to do so.*

This legislation would clearly demand a charge when applied to a minor self-producing an indecent image. If we consider Foucault's views of the role of the police (Foucault, 1975), he recognises their role as part of the punitive, rather than restorative, process—they collect evidence, they enforce the law and facilitate the punishment considered appropriate by society. It is not down to the enforcers of the law to make subjective judgements and whether the law is an ass.

While the legislation was updated in:

- s45 Sexual Offences Act 2003 (UK Government, 2003)

Which extended the law such that the subject of the image could be under 18, from the previous under sixteen, therefore aligning with the age of majority rather than the age of consent.

And was updated further with

- s67 Serious Crime Act 2015 (UK Government, 2015)

Which introduced new legislation making it a specific crime for an adult (18 and over) to engage in sexual communication with a child (under 16). Therefore, a minor requesting an intimate image from another minor would not be subject to this legislation. However, a minor responding to that request and sending them the requested image, would be.

Nevertheless, the fundamental act of production and distribution of an indecent image of a minor remained connected with the 1978 legislation and remains the key piece of legislation applied to legal debates regarding teen sexting in the UK.

This legislation makes it illegal for someone to produce, possess or distribute an indecent image of a child. Clearly in the event of self-generation and sharing, the victim will also be the perpetrator under this legislation. The legislation was introduced and debated at a time before the day when someone might self-generate an indecent image of themselves from their bedroom and have it passed around many recipients with the touch of a button could have ever been envisioned. However, in the modern digital world, we have legislation tension between on the one hand protecting the victim and on the other hand addressing the illegality of the generation and sharing. Those who produce images of themselves and send them to others, sometimes voluntarily, sometimes as a result of pressure or coercion (UK Safer Internet Centre et al., 2017), risk criminalisation should knowledge of this self-generation be made public and reported to the police.

While many instances of youth exchange of intimate images, the sharing and possession remained private, as we have discussed in previous chapters there are many occurrences where they went further. And as a result of further distribution, some victims were abused or pressured into other harmful behaviours (Phippen, 2016). However, in cases where those same vulnerable victims, whose rights under the UN Convention of the Rights of the Children (Article 34—Sexual Exploitation) should be protected from all forms of sexual abuse and exploitation, disclosed to adults with responsibilities for safeguarding, whether these be parents, school staff or social care professionals, it was likely, due to the legality of the act of production and distribution, that police would also become involved. We have certainly heard of incidents where, as a result of disclosure, the young person is subject to devise searches by adult safeguarding professionals which, as an act in itself would surely breach a number of rights including Article 16 (Right to Privacy) and potentially Article 37 (inhumane treatment). While we have already touched upon data protection tensions with safeguarding, we would question all but the most sensitive inspection of devices in these cases. Regardless of the form of investigation, it remains likely that, should s1 of the Protection of Children Act 1978 be applied as it is written, the young person risks further harm as a result of criminal records checks in the adult lives.

However, given the year that the law reached ascent, it could not have been in the minds of the legislators that the subject of the image, the taker of the image and the distributor of the image, could all be the same person. The motivation for the legislation arose from the somewhat notorious "obscenity campaigner", Mary Whitehouse (Thompson, 2012) whose lobbying focussed upon the protection of children from the organisation the opening operated in the UK in the 1970s, such as the

Paedophile Information Exchange (PIE),[4] an organisation who "openly campaigned for the lowering of the age of consent and made concerted efforts to normalise and justify sexual relationships between adults and children". Indeed, in an interview in the Guardian on 19 May 1977, Mrs Whitehouse stated

> *This, is the twentieth century manifestation of the slave trade, of the industrial exploitation of children in the last century. It is the exploitation of human beings in its lowest and most complete form. It is an attempt to justify the use of children for adult sexual gratification. The effect on, say, an eight year old child is impossible to conceive, especially we consider the physical and social maturity of the child.*[5]

Unsurprisingly, there was no mention in this time of minor-on-minor exchange of intimate images in Mrs Whitehouse's lobbying, the focus was solely on adults who exploit children. This lobbying resulted in a Private Member's Bill by the Bexeley Member of Parliament Cyril Townsend, whose obituary by former MP Tam Dalyell,[6] specifically states that:

> *He was prescient in his worries about child pornography and the sexual exploitation of children and in 1978 secured the passage into law of a private member's bill on the Protection of Children.*

The title of the bill makes it clear this piece of legislation is intended to protect children, in the case of the bill from the exploitation of children in the production of pornography by adult abusers. In its introduction to the House of Commons, Mr Townsend stated:

[4] See https://www.iicsa.org.uk/reports-recommendations/publications/investigation/westminster/part-g-paedophile-information-exchange/g1-introduction. Accessed January 2023.

[5] A scan of an article from the Guardian on the Paedophile Information Exchange quoting Mrs Whitehouse: https://spotlightonabuse.files.wordpress.com/2014/04/g190577.jpg. Accessed January 2023.

[6] See https://www.independent.co.uk/news/obituaries/sir-cyril-townsend-member-of-parliament-8974043.html. Accessed January 2023.

> *We acted to prevent abuse of little children as chimney sweeps and in the factories. We acted to prevent their abuse in dark satanic mills and deep down in the mines. Shall we act today to prevent their abuse in child pornography?*[7]

Clearly, the intention is to protect children from exploitation. While the debates around the bill were long and detailed (explored in more detail in Phippen & Brennan, 2020) at no point in the discussions was it suggested that this might be something enacted upon a minor from another minor or that the subject of the image was also the taker and distributor of the image. In the late 1970s, there is no reason to suggest anyone entertained the idea that in the future technology would be sufficiently advanced for an individual to take an intimate image of themselves and distribute it to peers using mass communication networks.

Indeed, if one explores Hansard to review the debate around the development of the bill, the focus was on the protection of children from exploitation by adult pornographers. In his introduction of the Bill before Parliament, Mr Townsend very clearly specified this legislation was to tackle the production of child pornography:

> Mr. Cyril D. Townsend (Bexleyheath)[8]
> *Child pornography is a distasteful subject to debate. Not unnaturally, the vast majority of our fellow countrymen are not fully aware of its prevalence in these islands, for much of the trade is kept under the counter. But right hon. and hon. Members appreciate from their postbags that there is much growing public anxiety and strong pressure for legislation action. Half a million people have already signed a petition calling for a change in the law. We have a duty to look into the sewers of our society. We have a duty to provide penalties for those who abuse our tolerance and our freedoms. Above all, we have a duty to protect innocent children.*

Within the debate, the focus is entirely on protecting children from abuse and exploitation in the production of pornography:

[7] Hansard. 10 February 1978. Volume 943. Column 1841. https://hansard.parliament.uk//Commons/1978-02-10/debates/d8d6a02b-8dab-4cde-8f05-3cbb1326f710/ProtectionOfChildrenBill#contribution-83f95c97-cc42-4eb5-b475-ebb2905662ef.

[8] Hansard. 10 February 1978. Volume 943. Column 1827. https://hansard.parliament.uk/Commons/1978-02-10/debates/d8d6a02b-8dab-4cde-8f05-3cbb1326f710/ProtectionOfChildrenBill#contribution-df8250b1-5615-435b-9e47-10dbc6d0465b. Accessed January 2023.

Rev. Ian Paisley (Antrim, North)[9]
The House should keep before it the fact that we are dealing with the welfare of the child. This is not a debate on pornography per se; *it is a debate on the taking of a child and the ruining of it for financial purposes so that the child's future is so twisted and warped that it is destroyed in time and eternity.*

Mr. Robert Hicks (Bodmin)[10]
On this occasion I wish my hon. Friend the Member for Bexleyheath every good fortune in his second attempt to get a Private Member's Bill on the statute book. His choice of subject reflects a widespread public concern. In the seven years that I have been a Member of this House I can recall only one previous occasion on which I have had as many letters and petitions on a social issue. The previous occasion had to do with the Abortion (Amendment) Bill in 1971.

I appreciate that there are widely differing attitudes towards pornography generally. On the other hand, no one in the House dissents from the proposition that children should not be involved at any stage, since they are specially vulnerable and are not able fully to realise what they are doing or consent to what they do when involved in this despicable activity. At times I find difficulty in defining my attitude towards those areas and instances where legislation should be introduced to protect people against themselves and their own actions. This is very much a grey area, as has been suggested. In terms of the exploitation of children I find myself in no such difficulty

Mr George Rogers (Chorely)[11]
The purpose of the Bill is to stop up the loopholes in the laws which are designed to protect children from abuse. It is apparent that the measure has generated

[9] Hansard. 10 February 1978. Volume 943. Column 1867. https://hansard.parliament.uk/Commons/1978-02-10/debates/d8d6a02b-8dab-4cde-8f05-3cbb1326f710/ProtectionOfChildrenBill#contribution-dc8f9f7f-8703-4d46-b794-a055f08a5a48. Accessed January 2023.

[10] Hansard. 10 February 1978. Volume 943. Column 1889. https://hansard.parliament.uk/Commons/1978-02-10/debates/d8d6a02b-8dab-4cde-8f05-3cbb1326f710/ProtectionOfChildrenBill#contribution-1685c107-4aca-4ed5-b36c-0e472b738906. Accessed January 2023.

[11] Hansard. 10 February 1978. Volume 943. Column 1885. https://hansard.parliament.uk/Commons/1978-02-10/debates/d8d6a02b-8dab-4cde-8f05-3cbb1326f710/ProtectionOfChildrenBill#contribution-ce2b312a-b49b-45cd-88bf-ae23531b33f5. Accessed January 2023.

> *wide support inside and outside the Chamber. The opening words of the Bill carry, for me at least, a deep appeal. They read:*
>
> > *"A Bill to prevent the exploitation of children."*
> > *I find that immensely heart-warming.*

As we can see from the above quote (our emphasis), it was clear in this debate that the protection of children from abuse was the motivation for the development of legislation. However, it is now being applied in cases where a minor might voluntarily exchange intimate images (that they have produced) with a partner, with no abuse occurring. However, should these images be non-consensually shared, and the victim subject to emotional abuse as a result, in what way is the modern-day application of this legislation protecting minors from abuse. Quite the opposite, in fact, as we have highlighted in disclosures from the Everyone's Invited website in Chapter 2—the law can be used to intensify the abuse, rather than protect the minor from harm.

There was a similar focus when the bill reached debate in the House of Lords.

> The Earl of LONGFORD[12]
> *I should like to express great concern about the proposed new Clause 1(4)(a). I am not dealing with a narrow legal point but with quite a broad point. Some of your Lordships may have read what Mrs. Whitehouse wrote in The Times this morning. After all, she has some standing in this matter because she and our organisation were the initiators of a campaign against child pornography.*

> Lord ROBERTSON of OAKRIDGE[13]
> *I welcome this Bill because it recognises that boys and girls under 16 need protection from those who would exploit their vulnerability and abuse their trust. May I join in thanking those who identified the gap in the law protecting children in this respect, those who alerted and mobilised public*

[12] Hansard. 18 May 1978. Volume 392. Column 547. https://hansard.parliament.uk/Lords/1978-05-18/debates/e4a134af-5217-4d78-9016-a24b6e70f04b/ProtectionOfChildrenBill#contribution-24d4192a-dc8b-4835-b2ce-311fc304f9ee. Accessed January 2023.

[13] Hansard. 18 May 1978. Volume 392. Column 565. https://hansard.parliament.uk/Lords/1978-05-05/debates/00f10535-2097-4fbe-9b95-46db2f2d0416/ProtectionOfChildrenBill#contribution-0abd6ce7-6fa2-4981-af13-31d60609e121. Accessed January 2023.

opinion and those who reacted to this by assisting the passage of the Bill so far. May I take this chance to pay tribute to the noble Baroness, Lady Faithfull, for the way in which she introduced the Bill.

Viscount BARRINGTON[14]
The purpose of the Bill is to protect children, and I think that is the point we want to remember. As I said, children have always been here and have always needed protection. Without taking up too much of your Lordships' time, I would take you back to ancient Carthage, where children needed protection from being put into a furnace for the honour of Moloch, the god of power, or even as far back as the Shaftesbury Acts of the last century, when it took a very long time, with some opposition in your Lordships' House, to prevent children from working in factories—often with the consent of their parents—for I forget how many hours a day in circumstances that we need not go into now. That was sacrificing children to Mammon.

I think most of us would agree that both of those were wrong, but now—and I do not think there is any need to produce evidence here, though it can be produced —children are being sacrificed to the god of pornography and/or sex. I do not know who that is. Perhaps it is Eros. I doubt if it is Aphrodite. But there I do not doubt that the menace facing us at the moment is the flood of "liberalism", which is one word used, though speaking as a Liberal I dislike that use of the word.

While this is but a sample of quotations from the debates that lead to the ascent of the Protection of Children Act, they are illustrative of the cross party, and house, support for a piece of legislation that would protect children from exploitation by adults in the manufacture of pornography. However, in the present day, we have legislative tension between on the one hand protecting the victim and on the other hand addressing the illegality of the generation and sharing.

However, is a minor who chooses to self-produce an image and send it to another minor a victim of exploitation or one being abused in the production of pornography? Clearly, there are some scenarios when there might be coercion or threat in the minor making the image or video of themselves, but the law still calls for the producer of the image (the minor) to be prosecuted due to the wording of the legislation.

[14] Hansard. 18 May 1978. Volume 392. Column 572. https://hansard.parliament.uk/Lords/1978-05-05/debates/00f10535-2097-4fbe-9b95-46db2f2d0416/ProtectionOfChildrenBill#contribution-514a4446-c841-4ff4-91e3-363498ea1f69. Accessed January 2023.

While there have been few updates in legislation since the Serious Crime Act 2015 and, realistically, little update to legislation around the production and distribution of images of minors since the original act, it is worthwhile, prior to our exploration of other tools introduced into the criminal justice system to address the flaws in the legislation, to consider what has been promoted by some in government as the solution to online harms—the Online Safety Bill.

3.4 The Online Safety Bill 2023

At the time of writing (December 2022), the fate of the Online Safety Bill 2023[15] remains in balance, and is making slow progress through parliament, against a backdrop of concerns regarding overreach and efficacy (Phippen, 2022). However, given it reflects the most up-to-date view on political thinking on "online safety", it is worthy of consideration to explore whether, its goal to make the UK "the safest place to go online in the world",[16] had any progressive developments around teen sexting and how the law might support victims and ensure those who choose to non-consensually share are prosecuted. Indeed, in the early debates around the bill, this point was raised in the House of Commons:

> Geraint Davies[17]
> (Swansea West) (Lab/Co-op)
> *Five years ago, I introduced a private Member's Bill that would have made it illegal for explicit private and sexual pictures to be shared online without consent. Subsequently, a ban on so-called revenge porn was introduced. Thousands of victims are now coming forward to the police yet only a handful of cases are going to court because victims cannot have anonymity and have to prove malicious intent. Will the Minister ensure this is criminalised and that these obstacles are not in place, so that victims can get their just deserts and criminals can be punished?*

[15] At the time of writing (January 2023) the Online Safety Bill is still making its way through parliament and therefore difficult to provide a definitive reference. Currently the latest version of the bill can be found at https://bills.parliament.uk/bills/3137.

[16] See https://www.gov.uk/government/news/world-first-online-safety-laws-introduced-in-parliament. Accessed January 2023.

[17] Hansard. 13 February 2020. Volume 671. Column 980. https://hansard.parliament.uk/Commons/2020-02-13/debates/A5CF7D6C-ECF0-459E-AE73-6D810E794236/OnlineHarmsLegislation.

Matt Warman
The hon. Member is right. Whether it is sexting or revenge porn, far too much has happened since his private Member's Bill that has not been positive. Our proposed legislation will be one way of tackling a part of that, but other important complementary pieces of draft legislation, to be introduced via *the Ministry of Justice and the Home Office, will close all the loopholes with regard to the kind of behaviour he mentions.*

However, the nature of the bill gives little room to consider peer-on-peer abuse resulting from the exchange of private images. Its focus seems almost entirely on a novel model for technology regulation, underpinned with a "duty of care", whereby legislators do not try to control the technology of itself, but place the responsibility for ensuring the technology is "safe" in the hands of the providers. This duty of care is enforced with the establishment of a regulator, who will have powers to assess this duty and impose fines and potentially further prosecution should the companies be found lacking. The motivation of the bill, it seems, centres on the regulation of platforms, rather than supporting the end user/victim of abuse.

At the committee stage of the reading of the bill (Joint Committee on the Draft Online Safety Bill, 2021), this intention was made clear, with the opening statement from the report published by the committee stating:

Big tech has failed its chance to self-regulate
The Online Safety Bill is the Government's chance to make the internet safer for all

Yet safety, it seems, must come at the hands of the platforms, rather than effective laws to protect victims of abuse and, perhaps, modify existing legislation that is now applied in manners for which it was never intended and, as a result, is creating a generation too scared to disclose harm as a result of non-consensual sharing.

3.5 Conclusion

As we have hopefully expressed strongly, it is clear that the legislative tools available to those with responsibilities for youth safeguarding are not fit for purpose when tackling this modern-day digital social phenomenon. In the next chapter, we will explore the introduction of what we might refer to as sticking plasters to try to address these problems outside of changes to the law. However, while done for the best of intentions and, we might suggest, mindful of the rights of the child, we will move to explore the impact of these measures and whether the impact was, indeed, a positive one.

References

Australian Government. (1995). *Criminal Code Act*. https://www.legislation.gov.au/Details/C2021C00183/Html/Volume_2. Accessed January 2023.

Bond, E. (2011). The mobile phone = bike shed? Children, sex and mobile phones. *New Media & Society*, *13*(4), 587–604.

Covell, K., Hoew, R. B., & McGillivray, A. (2017). Implementing children's education rights in schools. In M. D. Ruck, M. Peterson-Badali, & M. Freeman (Eds.), *Handbook of children's rights global and multidisciplinary perspectives* (pp. 296–311). Routledge.

Crofts, T., & Lievens, E. (2018). Sexting and the law. In M. Walgrave, J. Van Ouytsel, J. Ponnet, & J. R. Temple (Eds.), *Sexting: Motives and risks in online sexual self-presentation* (pp. 119–136). Palgrave Macmillan.

European Parliament. (2011). *Directive 2011/92/EU of the European Parliament and the of 13 December 2011 on combating the sexual abuse and sexual exploitation of children and child pornography, and replacing Council Framework Decision 2004/68/JHA*.

Foucault, M. (1975). *Discipline and punish* (A. Sheridan, Trans.). Edrtions Gallimar.

Joint Committee on the Draft Online Safety Bill. (2021). *Big tech has failed its chance to self-regulate*. https://ukparliament.shorthandstories.com/draft-online-safety-bill-joint-committee-report/index.html. Accessed January 2023.

Kettleborough, D. (2015). What's wrong with "child pornography"? The impact of terminology. Retrieved August, 2, 2017.

Lee, M., Crofts, T., McGovern, A., & Milivojevic, S. (2015). Sexting among young people: Perceptions and practices. *Trends and Issues in Crime and Criminal Justice*, (508), 1–9.

O'Connor, B. (2010, March 9). *Debate on Crimes Legislation Amendment (Sexual Offences Against Children) Bill 2010, Commonwealth, Parliamentary Debates, House of Representatives*, p. 2052.

Phippen, A. (2016). *Children's online behaviour and safety: Policy and rights challenges*. Springer.

Phippen, A. (2022). 'Evidence' based policy forming: The Joint Committee response to the draft Online Safety Bill. *Entertainment Law Review*, *33*(3), 81–88.

Phippen, A., & Brennan, M. (2020). *Sexting and revenge pornography: Legislative and social dimensions of a modern digital phenomenon*. Routledge.
Sacco, D., Argudin, R., Maguire, J., & Tallon, K. (2010). *Sexting: Youth practices and legal implications*. Berkman Center Research Publication (2010-8).
Slane, A. (2013). Sexting and the law in Canada. *The Canadian Journal of Human Sexuality, 22*(3), 117–122.
Sweeny, J. (2013). Sexting and freedom of expression: A comparative approach. *Kentucky Law Journal, 102*, 103.
Thompson, B. (2012). *Ban this Filth—Letters from the Mary Whitehouse Archive*. Faber and Faber.
UK Government. (1982). *Civic Government (Scotland) Act 1982*. https://www.legislation.gov.uk/ukpga/1982/45/contents. Accessed January 2023.
UK Government. (2003). *Section 45, Sexual Offences Act 2003*. https://www.legislation.gov.uk/ukpga/2003/42/section/45. Accessed January 2023.
UK Government. (2015). *Section 67, Serious Crime Act 2015*. https://www.legislation.gov.uk/ukpga/2015/9/section/67. Accessed January 2023.
UK Government. (2021). *Domestic Abuse Act 2021*. https://www.legislation.gov.uk/ukpga/2021/17/contents/enacted
UK Safer Internet Centre, Netsafe New Zealand, Office of the Australian eSafety Commissioner. (2017). *Young people and sexting—Attitudes and behaviours*. https://www.esafety.gov.au/-/media/cesc/documents/corporate-office/young_people_and_sexting_attitudes_and_behaviours_pdf.pdf
United Nations. (1989). *United Nations Convention on the Rights of the Child*. https://www.unicef.org.uk/what-we-do/un-convention-child-rights/. Accessed January 2023.

CHAPTER 4

Understanding the Police Response: Putting Sticking Plasters over Legislation

Abstract In exploring the realities of policing teen sexting, we explore the policy developments and changes in policing practice that have followed the emergence of the exchange of intimate images by minors, from the application of the legislation, through the advent of "Outcome 21" interventions, to the more recent diversionary approach afforded by "Outcome 22" crime recording. We show through data that the law and these policy developments are applied inconsistently across the country, resulting in random outcomes for victims of non-consensual sharing of images among minors, depending on location, intervention and the individual awareness of any given police officer.

Keywords Teen sexting · Policing · Outcome 21 · Outcome 22 · Diversion

4.1 Introduction

This chapter provides an analysis of both Ministry of Justice data around the application of section 1 of the PCA 1978 to minors, and Freedom of Information data collected in three parts, over three years, by the authors, that looks at police arrest data and the application of Outcome 21 and 22

A. Phippen and E. Bond, *Policing Teen Sexting*, Palgrave's Critical Policing Studies, https://doi.org/10.1007/978-3-031-31455-1_4

responses to these arrests. It will highlight that, regardless of CPS and CoP guidance, minors are still being arrested and charged as a result of sexting incidents, and that outcome recording can be very variable across force areas. As a result of the data collected, this chapter will discuss both the challenges for policing these behaviours, and also the impact of inconsistent practice upon young people's rights, particularly when compared to the application of alternative legislation to adults.

4.2 The Application of Sticking Plasters

In the previous chapters, we have presented a strong case for the widespread impacts of applying legislation developed for one social ill to be applied to another, unimagined at the time of ascent, collection of behaviours and acts which can have significant impacts upon young people but, in a lot of cases, form part of twenty-first-century relationships. The youth voice strongly shows us that this prohibitive approach to what they see, in the majority of cases, as not being harmful, results in further harm, rather than better outcomes, and we have shown the intentions of the legislators who developed the legislation had no perception of how it might be applied forty years after it was introduced. In this chapter, we explore what has happened as a result of the acknowledged challenges of policing this problematic area of law and how these approaches have, in reality, been applied. In doing so we consider the central thread of the arguments made in this book—are outcomes for young people improved as a result of these interventions.

While the law remains the same, that is not to say that the criminal justice system has not been mindful of the problems with the application of the Protection of Children Act 1978 to sexting incidents and the unwanted criminalisation of minors as a result. As a result of high-profile cases (for example[1]) and resultant media pressure that the criminalisation of a minor for the self-generation of an indecent image seemed disproportionate, we saw a chain of responses from actors in the criminal justice system to try to reduce the risk of arrest and move to prosecute as a result of a consensual incident.

However, we should note that the first of these interventions, by the Crown Prosecution Service (the organisation ultimately responsible for

[1] See https://www.telegraph.co.uk/news/uknews/crime/11840985/Teenage-boy-added-to-police-database-for-sexting.html.

analysing police investigations and deciding whether the proceed with prosecution) took place in 2015, four years after the introduction of EU Directive 2011/93/EU (ibid.) which, as we have noted in the previous chapter, provided a means of exemption, should a member state choose it, when applying state child pornography legislation to consensual image exchanges by minors. We can conclude, therefore, that the UK chose not to apply these exemptions.

With the introduction of the new Revenge Pornography laws in 2015 (Section 33 Criminal Justice and Courts Act 2015—UK Government, 2015), the Crown Prosecution Service publish guidance (Crown Prosecution Service, 2017) on how the legislation should be applied. In this guidance, the CPS recognised the cross over with s1 Protection of Children Act 1978, and introduced the value of prosecution of minors under public interest:

> *Where images may have been taken when the victim was under 18, prosecutors should consider whether any offences under section 1 of the Protection of Children Act 1978 (taking, distributing, possessing or publishing indecent photographs of a child) or under section 160 of the Criminal Justice Act 1988 (possession of an indecent photograph of a child) have been committed.*

After expressing this "letter of the law" perspective, the advice becomes more pragmatic:

> *However, care should be taken when considering any cases of 'sexting' that involve images taken of persons under 18. Sexting commonly refers to the sharing of illicit images, videos or other content between two or more persons. Sexting can cover a broad range of activities, from the consensual sharing of an image between two children of a similar age in a relationship to instances of children being exploited, groomed, and bullied into sharing images, which in turn may be shared with peers or adults without their consent.*
>
> *Whilst it would not usually be in the public interest to prosecute the consensual sharing of an image between two children of a similar age in a relationship, a prosecution may be appropriate in other scenarios. In addition to the offences outlined above, consideration may be given to the offence of Causing or inciting a child to engage in sexual activity under section 8 (child under 13) or section 10 (child) of the Sexual Offences Act 2003 (SOA).*

Therefore, while there was an unwillingness to change the law, it was at least acknowledged by the prosecutor that it is not often in the public interest to prosecute a minor for the self-production and consensual sharing of an intimate image.

Further updates to guidance around indecent images of children by the CPS in 2018 (updated 2020) (Crown Prosecution Service, 2020) reinforced the public interest point:

> *Prosecutors should consider whether a prosecution is required in the public interest and/or whether an out of court disposal is appropriate, where youth offenders are concerned, applying the CPS guidance on Youth Offenders. This is particularly the case where children make and/or share images of themselves, depending on the circumstance*

In the winter of 2016, influenced in part by media pressure and also CPS guidance, in order to hopefully provide a more consistent response from the police, the College of Policing (2016) issued its own guidance, which allows a sexting incident to be reported and recorded, without the child ending up with a criminal record. In order to provide a middle ground between the incident going unreported, and the image producer/victim ending up with a criminal record, guidance was issued on something referred to as an "Outcome 21" response:

> *Further investigation, resulting from the crime report, which could provide evidence sufficient to support formal action being taken against the suspect is not in the public interest – police decision.*

This would, in theory, shut down any need for investigation and ensure that the child would not be arrested, should the conclusion that no coercion or aggravating factor was evidence:

> *Outcome 21 may be considered the most appropriate resolution in youth produced sexual imagery cases where the making and sharing is considered non-abusive and there is no evidence of exploitation, grooming, profit motive, malicious intent (e.g. extensive or inappropriate sharing (e.g. uploading onto a pornographic website) or it being persistent behaviour. Where these factors are present, outcome 21 would not apply.*

This development was viewed as a progressive step forward in policing, while still being constrained by the limitations of the legislation. However, this did place to decision on whether to record as an Outcome 22, or move to arrest, down to the officer. And therefore requires up-to-date training and sensitivity around the issues. Which can be a challenge when engaged in policing, as evidenced by Tyrrell et al. (2017). However, "Outcome 21" was heralded as a progressive solution to the challenges of policing teen sexting and would result in the young person not ending up with a criminal record for something that, if they were to do in post-age of majority, they would be protected from abuse. However, further reading of the guidance raised some concerns this would not necessarily be the case. In the guidance it was suggested that the following is read out to the child and/or parents to clarify the use of the Outcome 21 recording:

> *You/Your child has been recorded on police systems against (add crime type) in line with Home Office crime recording rules. After consideration of all relevant factors, a decision has been made that no further action will be taken by the police in this instance. <Your child> has not been convicted or cautioned for any offence connected with this investigation.*
>
> *In the event that a future 'Enhanced Disclosure and Barring Service' (DBS) check is required it is unlikely that this record will be disclosed unless you/your child are investigated or have further action taken against you/them in the future which could suggest a relevant pattern of behaviour.*
>
> *Any decision to disclose will be made by the chief police officer dealing with the request, based on all factors and information available at the time of the decision.*

This would suggest that while it is unlikely that such a recorded incident would resurface in later life, it was not the case that the incident would simply disappear.

We also noted that, even when we visited schools after Outcome 21 was introduced, the educational messages were still prohibitive and basic—don't send nudes, it's illegal. Since the introduction of Outcome 21 in 2016, we have never visited a school where a more nuanced discussion around the law and outcome recording, and what public interest is, is delivered within the educational message. More simple, it would seem, to maintain the prohibitive message.

In the evolution of the application of criminal justice outcomes, we started to also see the application of "Outcome 22" recording to teen sexting.

Outcome 22 is a different approach to the application of Outcome 21. Guidance produced by the National Police Chief's Council in 2019[2] defined Outcome 22 as:

> *Outcome Type 22:*
> *Diversionary, educational or intervention activity, resulting from the crime report, has been undertaken and it is not in the public interest to take any further action.*
>
> *Detail required for Outcome 22:*
> *Decision making should be clearly documented as to what education and diversionary activityhas been put in place to address the suspects offending behaviour and why the OIC believes this is a more effective outcome than out of court disposals or charge*

Furthermore, Outcome 22 was a general "outcome" that could be recorded against all manner of crimes, it was not specifically developed for teen sexting. It was viewed as means to deal with low-level crimes where the use of a "diversionary activity" could be used so that no further action needed to take place. However, there was little detailed guidance on what that diversion might look like. The guidance gave examples:

> *E.g. attendance at victim awareness course, drug awareness course, engagement with addiction services, voluntary referral to da perpetrator programme.*

But little more detail than that regarding how a diversion might be developed and, in the case of an educational intervention, who might develop this.

It is interesting to note that the early guidance, it specifically refers to education interventions for low-level sexual offences. However, it explicitly states that it should not be applied in teen sexting cases:

> *Low level sexual offences where education is provided as a result of the investigation but no formal outcome is given.... (NB: this is not intended to replicate Outcome 21. Youth produced sexual imagery should be dealt with in accordance with existing O21 guidance).*

[2] See https://justiceinnovation.org/sites/default/files/media/document/2021/outcome_22_-_npcc_briefing_note_v1_march_2019.pdf. Accessed January 2023.

This did immediately raise a question regarding why we were hearing of incidents of Outcome 22 being used for this very purpose, given the guidance was clear it should not be. There was no further rationale for why Outcome 22 should not be used, just that it should not be. Which, given the calls from young people for educational support around these issues, rather than legal threats, was somewhat confusing. It would seem in some instances that it would be an ideal application of the intervention, with appropriate guidance on how the said intervention might be developed. Young people were not calling for "any" education, they were calling for education delivered by professionals who understood the issues and listened to their concerns.

More recent Outcome 22 guidance perhaps confuses things further. While providing more detail on when to apply Outcome 22, with further examples of good practice for those involved in the development of diversions, there is more confusion around teen sexting. On page 10 of the guidance it is stated:

> *Low level sexual offences where education is provided as a result of the investigation but no formal outcome is given. (NB: this is not intended to replicate Outcome 21. Youth produced sexual imagery should be dealt with in accordance with existing O21 guidance).*

However, on the following page, with specific mention of "Youth produced sexual imagery", the guidance states:

> *Outcome 21 should be used in these instances. However, should other interventions or diversionary activity be put in place, then O22 may be considered appropriate.*
>
> *In January 2016 the Home Office launched a new outcome code (Outcome 21) to help, in part, formalise the discretion available to the police relating to the handling of crimes such as youth produced sexualised imagery.*
>
> *A key objective of the Police guidance was to outline a proportionate response to investigating youth produced sexual imagery which in turn reduces the potential over criminalisation of children through Outcome 21*

It seems to say "you should use Outcome 21, but if you can think of appropriate interventions of diversions, you can use Outcome 22".

All of the above measures have been developed entirely because the law has not been updated to embrace modern society. While developed with the best of intentions we can see that if the guidance is considered on the whole, it can be quite a confusing picture.

4.3 What Does This Mean for Young People?

We were told that these measures were introduced to ensure that young people would no longer be prosecuted for the consensual sharing of images, unless there were mitigating factors. However, data from the Ministry of Justice (2022), shown in Table 4.1—Prosecutions of minors charged under section 1 of the Protection of Children Act (source: Ministry of Justice, 2022), highlight that the law (specifically section 1 of the Protection of Children Act) was still being applied to proceed against and prosecute minors:

Which would suggest that in some cases young people were still being prosecuted under this legislation.

Of course, one would hope that those that reach the courts have been checked for evidence and public interest and it is difficult to ascertain with this simple quantitative data whether these cases were more coercive or abusive in nature (or, indeed, refer to possession of other child abuse material by a minor).

However, given there was little reduction in proceeding against after the introduction of both Outcome 21 (in 2016) and Outcome 22 (in 2019), we felt these figures deserved further investigation.

Clearly, it is not possible to carry out a detailed examination of criminal justice records due to the sensitive personal nature of a lot of the data. However, police forces in the UK are liable, as public bodies, to Freedom of Information requests under the Freedom of Information Act 2000 (UK Government, 2000). This allows members of the public to ask questions of public organisations and, where appropriate, receive information that is posted into the public domain about these questions.

As such, we have issued two Freedom of Information requests on police forces. One in 2019, to explore the introduction of Outcome 21, and one in 2022 to investigate the impact of Outcome 22.

Both requests asked for information on crime recording of minors against Home Office Crime Code 86/2, which relates specifically to s1 Protection of Children Act 1978.

The first request, in 2019, was worded thus:

Table 4.1 Prosecutions of minors charged under section 1 of the Protection of Children Act

	2008	*2009*	*2010*	*2011*	*2012*	*2013*	*2014*	*2015*	*2016*	*2017*	*2018*	*2019*	*2020*	*2021*
Proceeded against	39	41	41	40	34	40	50	56	61	55	45	42	43	59
Convicted	33	33	36	37	26	30	39	48	56	39	41	32	36	49
Sentenced	33	33	36	36	27	30	39	49	54	41	41	32	37	48

Source Ministry of Justice (2022)

(a) *Please could you provide details of the number of arrests related to the taking, making or distribution of an indecent (or pseudo sexual) image of a child (home office code 86/2) where suspect was under the age of 18 since December 2016.*
(b) *If you hold the information, please could you also provide details of the number of arrests related to the taking, making or distribution of an indecent (or pseudo sexual) image of a child (home office code 86/2) where suspect was under the age of 14 since December 2016.*
(c) *Please could you provide the total number of crimes related to the taking, making or distribution of an indecent (or pseudo sexual) image of a child (home office code 86/2) where suspect was under 18 that have been recorded as Outcome 21, since December 2016.*
(d) *If you hold the information, please could you also provide the total number of crimes related to the taking, making or distribution of an indecent (or pseudo sexual) image of a child (home office code 86/2) where suspect was under the age of 14 that have been recorded as Outcome 21 since December 2016.*

We specifically asked for data for those under 14, as well as under 18, to determine whether those who were pre-teen, or barely teenagers, were being arrested under this legislation and whether outcome 21 was being applied in these cases.

We would acknowledge that, as with any Freedom of Information request related to crime data held, the response will not allow us to explore the context of activity, for example, differentiating between those who might have self-generated, those who might have shared self-generated images, and those who might have accessed indecent images of minors online. We also acknowledge that, as with any crime data, the context of the crime is not known and therefore specific inference to behaviours cannot be made.

However, Freedom of Information data is useful to look broadly at practice across different forces to determine the consistency of approach and, specifically in this case, whether Outcome 21 is being applied consistently, which was very much our goal with this first request. Given we had no evidence of a reduction in prosecutions since the introduction of these measures, we wanted to understand how they were being used.

After a period of 3 months (far in excess of the 20-day period public bodies are, by law, expected to respond to a Freedom of Information request) we received useful responses from 30 forces. In addition to these responses, we also had two response with no data, and 3 forces claiming exemption under section 12(1) of the Freedom of Information Act.[3] This, given that we had received responses from 32 forces that we could process, does highlight differences in both crime recording and processing across different organisations. We should also note that for two responses we were informed that the force does not store Outcome 21 recording information, which again highlights an inconsistency of recording that makes informing national policy complex.

Due to differences in recording and retrieval, we are mindful (and indeed were reminded of such in a number of responses) that we should not directly compare responses from different forces. This is a reasonable request given the differences in recording systems and information retrieval. Therefore, while we present response data in tabular forms to illustrate types of response, we are mindful that we only use data specific to forces to generate further statistics and only draw general conclusions from our analysis. We have also not named forces in this reporting, as there is nothing to be gained from this holistic analysis from "naming and shaming". Our interest was in the consistency of practice and recording, not playing forces off against each other or ranking performance.

For the 2019 request, results shown in Table 4.2, we have also aggregated under 14 and under 18 data as we did not differentiate this for the 2022 request.

What is clear from these results is:

- Children and young people are still being arrested under crime code 86/2
- Outcome 21 recording is being applied by most forces, to varying levels
- The number of Outcome 21 recordings, in more cases, far exceeds the number of arrests, which is, superficially, a positive thing.

A scatter plot is a useful tool to visually explore these data. While we are mindful to caveat this presentation with an acknowledgement that presenting two discrete variables to represent what is in reality a complex social system, and would not expect to see a perfect relationship between

[3] The processing of the request would be too time-consuming or costly to the organisation to fall under the expectations of the act.

Table 4.2 Arrest and Outcome 21 recording from Home Office crime code 86/2 from 30 police forces

	Arrests	*OC21*
Force A	8	155
Force B	2	96
Force C	10	51
Force D	4	10
Force E	3	2
Force F	10	504
Force G	2	146
Force H	2	103
Force I	3	10
Force J	7	109
Force K	9	909
Force L	4	0
Force M	16	2
Force N	5	184
Force O	18	134
Force P	8	128
Force Q	7	288
Force R	6	122
Force S	112	220
Force T	14	135
Force U	20	2
Force V	0	2
Force W	5	659
Force X	18	166
Force Y	11	119
Force Z	17	484
Force AA	1	107
Force BB	8	170
Force CC	15	520
Force DD	8	0

Source Authors' Freedom of Information request

the two variables (because each disclosed crime or incident has a unique set of causal factors) we would, should practice be consistent across regions, at least see some relationship between volume of arrests to Outcome 21s. However, as we can see from Fig. 4.1, this is certainly not the case.

So the data reports broadly that Outcome 21 has impacted across forces and is being used to record crimes without typical risk of criminalisation for young people. However, the data does also very clearly show

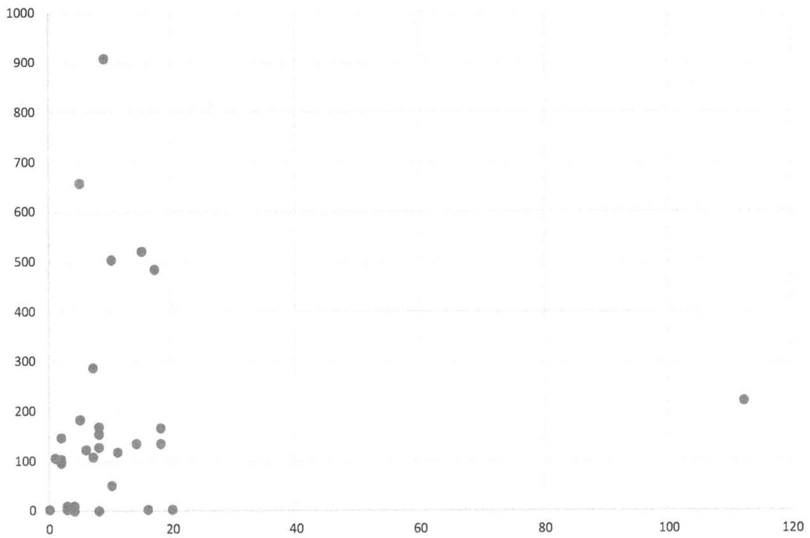

Fig. 4.1 A Scatter Plot of Arrests vs Outcome 21s issued

that it is not consistent practice across forces. In some cases the number of Outcome 21s recorded far exceeds the number of arrests, in others, arrests exceed Outcome 21s.

To reiterate, it is difficult to comment on specific cases because we cannot determine the nature of specific crimes and therefore the rationale for the use of Outcome 21 recording, we would, if we were to view Outcome 21 recording as a positive alternative to the criminalisation of minors, expect the proportion of arrests to Outcome 21 recording to be low. However, we can see with these data that while in most forces this is the case, there is also an example of the opposite, which suggests a minor is far more likely to be arrested for this sort of crime than receive an Outcome 21 recording. As such, the data also strongly highlights the inconsistencies of the application of Outcome 21 recording across forces.

Therefore, we can report a mixed picture regarding the challenges of policing youth involved in the possession and distribution of indecent images of minors, and the clear relationship between this and teen sexting. We can see that since the advent of Outcome 21 recording, some forces are applying this a great deal, which is preferable to arrest (albeit with the caveat that there are cases where the arrest of a minor for possession and distribution of indecent images of a minor is entirely valid, particularly if done with malicious intent or coercion).

The second request, which was placed in 2022, covering the time period July 2021 to July 22, aimed to determine a similar impact on the introduction of Outcome 22 recording, and also to consider whether there had been changes in practice since the original request in 2019 which measured the impact of the emergent Outcome 21 policy in 2016. This was particularly of interest given the NPCC guidance not (in general) to use Outcome 22 for teen sexting incidents. Should this advice have been consistently applied, we would have expected very low numbers of Outcome 22 recordings for our request.

The wording of the request was:

1. *Please could you provide details of the number of arrests related to the taking, making or distribution of an indecent (or pseudo sexual) image of a child (home office code 86/2) where suspect was under the age of 18 between 1st July 2021 and 1st July 2022.*
2. *Please could you provide the total number of crimes related to the taking, making or distribution of an indecent (or pseudo sexual) image of a child (home office code 86/2) where suspect was under 18 that have been recorded as Outcome 21, between 1st July 2021 and 1st July 2022.*
3. *Please could you provide the total number of crimes related to the taking, making or distribution of an indecent (or pseudo sexual) image of a child (home office code 86/2) where suspect was under 18 that have been recorded as Outcome 22, between 1st July 2021 and 1st July 2022.*
4. *If possible, and do disregard if this is too much trouble, if you have a published policy regarding when Outcome 21 and Outcome 22 are recorded related to the sharing of intimate images of a minor, please could you also provide this. I realise some forces might just follow NPCC guidance and not have their own policy.*

We asked specifically about the guidance used because we wanted to understand how forces applied the application of Outcome 22, which we will explore in more detail in Chapter 5.

The results, again, show inconsistency across forces, as shown in Table 4.3. The forces aliases do not necessarily compare to those reported in

Table 4.3 Arrest, Outcome 21 and Outcome 22 recording from Home Office crime code 86/2 from 33 police forces

	Arrests	*OC21*	*OC22*
Force A	1	302	23
Force B	251	111	11
Force C	6	27	47
Force D	3	214	7
Force E	5	18	20
Force F	5	139	15
Force G	9	201	5
Force H	12	174	16
Force I	3	23	3
Force J	0	0	0
Force K	243	76	8
Force L	9	101	0
Force M	24	235	52
Force N	1	0	0
Force O	10	145	2
Force P	93	280	9
Force Q	11	283	12
Force R	10	11	3
Force S	4	27	0
Force T	8	0	0
Force U	5	193	5
Force V	4	159	20
Force W	0	314	26
Force X	0	174	143
Force Y	0	34	4
Force Z	10	0	0
Force AA	11	88	2
Force BB	18	49	6
Force CC			
Force DD	2	93	5
Force EE	0	237	0
Force FF	6	181	1
Force GG	2	66	44

Source Authors' Freedom of Information request

the first round of requests, and we do not attempt to marry the two data sources together. However, what is clear is that in most cases forces are making large use of Outcome 21, and some Outcome 22. In one case, a force that did return in the first round of requests returned zero responses for all three categories, when they were, in the past arresting and making use of Outcome 21, which would suggest a force wide policy to no longer investigate minor on minor intimate image sharing. However, again, it is difficult to discover why from this data. There are other forces who equally return no arrests, which again suggests a change in policy but do, in contrast to Force J, still record as Outcome 21 and Outcome 22.

What this we might expect from these data, comparing proportions, again, shows little consistency of practice. Proportions vary wildly between forces but do show, in general Outcome 21 is used far more than Outcome 22. One other significant change was the number of forces that returned zero arrests during this period, which differs from the first set of data, which showed only one force having no arrests. While it is difficult to conclude from this result, it does at least highlight a trend to move away from arrests under this code when applied to minors.

To further illustrate the lack of consistent application of each type of intervention, we have a challenge with using a scatter plot given we have now introduced a new variable—Outcome 22s issued. However, a buddle plot (see Fig. 4.2) provides us with a useful tool to explore this. The x-axis of the graph measures Outcome 21s and the y-Outcome 22s. The size of

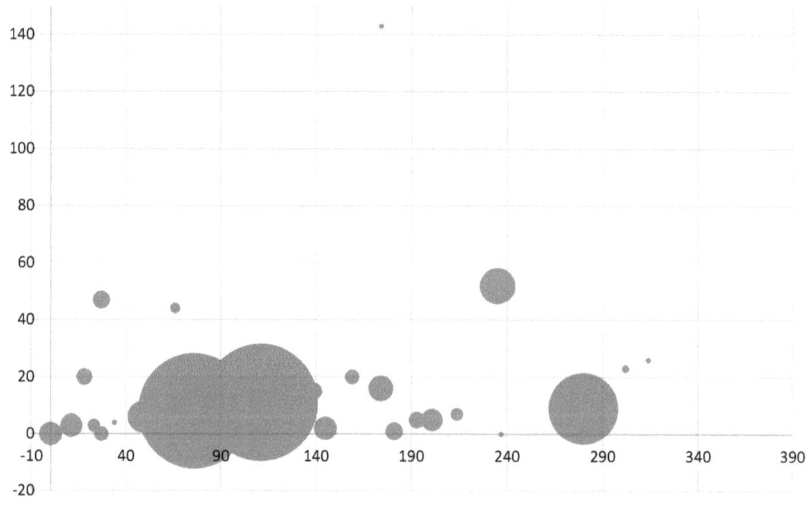

Fig. 4.2 A Bubble Plot showing volume of outcome 21s (x axis), 22s (y axis) and arrests (size)

each bubble[4] relates to arrests, so combined we have a strong visualisation of the relationship between arrests, Outcome 21s and Outcome 22s.

As with Fig. 4.1, what we can conclude from this visualisation is there is little consistency of practice, and forces are applying their own judgement on when to apply, with inconsistent results.

4.4 Conclusions

In this chapter, we have explored the measures introduced by actors in the criminal justice system to tackle the problems of the application of s1 Protection of Children Act 1978 to teen sexting incidents. By drawing up quantitative data we can see that there is a great deal of inconsistency in how the measures are applied, which does question how these measures, while perhaps developed with the best of intentions, impact upon young people within an overloaded and under-resourced justice system.

In the next chapter, we explore this from a qualitative perspective, drawing upon discussions with those involved in the criminal justice and youth justice processes to explore how these different outcomes are applied and how interventions are developed.

References

College of Policing. (2016). *Police action in response to youth produced sexual imagery ('Sexting')*. http://www.college.police.uk/News/College-news/Documents/Police_action_in_response_to_sexting_-_briefing_(003).pdf. Accessed December 2022.

Crown Prosecution Service. (2017). *Revenge Pornography—Guidelines on prosecuting the offence of disclosing private sexual photographs and films*. https://www.cps.gov.uk/legal-guidance/revenge-pornography-guidelines-prosecuting-offence-disclosing-private-sexual. Accessed December 2022.

Crown Prosecution Service. (2020). *Indecent and prohibited images of children*. https://www.cps.gov.uk/legal-guidance/indecent-and-prohibited-images-children. Accessed December 2022.

Ministry of Justice. (2022). *Criminal Justice System statistics quarterly: June 2022*. https://www.gov.uk/government/statistics/criminal-justice-system-statistics-quarterly-june-2022. Accessed January 2023.

[4] We have taken slight creative license with arrest data in order to be able to incorporate those forces who has no arrests. In these cases we have applied a fractional value to the arrest data so they are visible as the smallest bubbles on the plot.

Tyrrell, K., Bond, E., Manning, M., & Dogaru, C. (2017). *Diversion, prevention and youth justice: A model of integrated decision making: An evaluation of the Suffolk Youth Offending Service Diversion Programme*. University of Suffolk. https://www.uos.ac.uk/sites/default/files/Diversion%20Evalution%20Report%202017.pdf. Accessed January 2023.
UK Government. (2000). *Freedom of Information Act 2000*. https://www.legislation.gov.uk/ukpga/2000/36/contents. Accessed January 2023.
UK Government. (2015). *Section 33, Criminal Justice and Courts Act 2015*. legislation.gov.uk/ukpga/2015/2/section/33/enacted. Accessed January 2023.

CHAPTER 5

The Challenges of Diversionary Intervention

Abstract In exploring the grassroots of diversionary intervention, we explore, through discussion with safeguarding and policing professionals, the challenges of supporting young people within a framework of out-of-date legislation and poor national policy, to further highlight the need for new or updated legislation that is youth and victim-centric. Discussions show how diversions are constructed based upon poorly defined risk tools, poor or non-existent training and a lack of understanding of the context, with many professionals bringing their own biases to judging young people, rather than focussing upon the best interests of the child.

Keywords Teen sexting · Diversion · Fraser/Gillick Competence · Risk tools · Police training · Professional bias

5.1 Introduction

As we argue in Chapter 2, the debate surrounding childhood, sexuality and media is fraught with contradictions and anxieties associated with protecting children's sexual innocence (Jackson & Scott, 2004). This chapter develops the findings presented in Chapter 4 to explore why police responses can be so inconsistent and the challenges police and

A. Phippen and E. Bond, *Policing Teen Sexting*, Palgrave's Critical Policing Studies, https://doi.org/10.1007/978-3-031-31455-1_5

professionals within the criminal justice system experience in trying to apply this legislation that is both cognisant of the law and mindful of the needs of minors who have engaged in these practices and perhaps become victims of abuse as a result. In spite of the greater surveillance, control and regulation of children, there is an increasing tendency to recognise children as persons in their own right, as individuals with a capacity for self-realisation (a notion embraced by modernity) and, within the limits of social interdependency, autonomous action (Prout, 2000). Our discussion here draws upon the ethnographic work of the authors working with the police forces and youth justice professionals in different parts of the country, attempting to understand the choices that are made by police in considering when to arrest, charge or dispose different outcomes. In particular, the subjective disposal of Outcome 21 and 22 and the impact of this on young people's lives. In particular, the more recent application of Outcome 22 (diversionary or educational intervention) is explored to better understand who makes those decisions and how the interventions are developed and applied. It will also explore wider interventions by police around teen sexting (such as educational interventions) and how this aligns with wider education policy (such as Relationships and Sex Education statutory curriculum).

We would suggest that the processes in place to address these diversions, against a broader backdrop of what is sometimes referred to as "Out of court disposal", shows little cognisance for the young person as an individual in their own right, and more a part in a mechanical process that has to show response to a crime, and movement through the system, but with little thought to the individual circumstances of the young person or an evaluation of the efficacy of the intervention. We should also stress, prior to a more in-depth exploration of discussions with both police and youth justice practitioners, that our criticisms around lack of best interests are directed not at the individuals, but the process under which they make these decisions. We are confident that everyone we spoke to in the exploration of the nature of interventions concerning youth-produced imagery was aware of the nature of the behaviours, the issues with the legislation, and an eagerness to ensure, except for the most abusive of cases, that young people avoid the criminal justice system. However, they are held to account for the processes with which they have to work, and the support they receive from national coordination around criminal justice processes.

It is with these processes we would take issue. While we acknowledge the importance of having established policies and processes to ensure a consistent response to issues faced by those working in youth justice, we would argue that a process is not sufficient (and this is borne out by the discussions we have had).

5.2 A Criminal Justice Process

In the previous chapter, we explored the quantitative data on how police apply arrest and Outcome 21/22 practices to young produced intimate image exchange. The final question we asked in this request was whether each force had its own policy on the use of Outcome 21/22. Only two forces had their own policy, and most took NPCC/national guidance as the foundation of this.[1] Therefore, we will focus on national guidance when considering the application of these outcomes.

The Youth Justice Board's guidance (2019) on the application of out-of-court disposals has much detail on the process. For instance, at the start of the process:

> *To help decide the most appropriate out-of-court disposal for a child, you should first Undertake a screening process. this covers:*
>
> - *the likelihood of the child complying with the disposal*
> - *whether that would be the best way to encourage desistance*

Establishes that the professional should decide whether an out-of-court disposal is the best approach to "encourage desistance", which once again exhibits the prohibitive nature of a lot of the discourse around intervention. There is nothing in the guidance that explores whether such an outcome would be in the young person's best interests, just whether they will "comply" and "desist".

The guidance talks in a number of sections about a "Gravity" score, which will help professionals decide whether to apply an out-of-court disposal. This refers to the now somewhat (released in 2013) old Association of Chief Police Officers Gravity Matrix (Youth Justice Legal Centre, n.d.), a tool provided for professionals to allow them to make judgements

[1] With one further force refusing this request as it would take too long to discover whether they have a policy.

of the "gravity" of the offence and whether out-of-court disposal is appropriate. The gravity of the crime is rated from 1 to 4, with 1 being the least concerning and 4 essentially stating that the offender should be entered into the justice system:

> *Level 4—Normally result in charge.*
> *Level 2 to 3—Normally a youth caution. If the offending behaviour cannot be satisfactorily addressed by a caution consider Youth Conditional Caution. If neither of these address the offending behaviour or provides the necessary support then charge*
> *Level 1—Always the minimum response applicable to the individual offender, i.e. Community Resolution or caution, youth conditional caution or charge.*

Crimes are classified as a level starting point, and then aggravating or mitigating factors can either increase or decrease the rating. The matrix covers a wide rather of crimes, but has little detail in general around online harms, aside from some advice that most malicious communications are generally rated as level 2 as a starting point. However, there is specific coverage of crimes related to section 1 of the Protection of Children Act 1978 (ibid.). The first part of the advice is at least sufficiently progressive to acknowledge if a child had distributed images to an adult, this might be a result of abuse or coercion:

> *Where a youth Is In possession of pornographic Images the Involvement of any adult should be fully investigated, as the youth may be the victim of abuse or grooming. In such cases referral to social services may be more appropriate than criminal justice action.*

Certainly, the advice seems to focus on adult and child exchange, rather than acknowledging the application of the law to child-on-child exchange. Perhaps more concerning is that the Gravity Matrix, which we should remember is used as a default tool to decide upon the application of an out-of-court disposal (such as Outcome 21 or 22), places the starting gravity of any offence under section 1 of the Protection of Children Act as Level 3, one less than the most extreme rating. The guidance also defines a number of Aggravating Factors which could increase the level:

- Child under 13
- Large number of images
- Images are level 3 or above
- Images distributed
- Damage caused

"Images are level 3 or above" both reflect the age of the advice and relate to the derivation from the COPINE scale (Taylor et al., 2001) which was established in the case Regina V Oliver in 2002.[2]

Sometimes referred to as the SAP (Sentencing Advisory Panel) scale, it defines images against five levels:

1. Nudity or erotic posing with no sexual activity
2. Sexual activity between children, or solo masturbation by a child
3. Non-penetrative sexual activity between adult(s) and child(ren)
4. Penetrative sexual activity between child(ren) and adult(s)
5. Sadism or bestiality.

This categorisation has since been replaced by updated Sentencing Council guidance (2014) to three categories:

> *Category A—Possession of images involving penetrative sexual activity. Possession of images involving sexual activity with an animal or sadism. Sharing images involving penetrative sexual activity. Sharing images involving sexual activity with an animal or sadism. Creating images involving penetrative sexual activity. Creating images involving sexual activity with an animal or sadism.*
> *Category B—Possession of images involving non-penetrative sexual activity. Sharing of images involving non-penetrative sexual activity. Creating images involving non-penetrative sexual activity.*
> *Category C—Possession of other indecent images not falling within categories A or B. Sharing of other indecent images not falling within categories A or B. Creating other indecent images not falling within categories A or B.*

[2] [2002] EWCA Crim 2766, [2003] 2 Cr App R (S) 15.

Therefore, practitioners are once again faced with the application of incomplete or out-of-date advice to make decisions that will impact a young person's life. We would also dwell on the advice that distribution is a mitigating factor in the Gravity matrix, given the typical nature of the exchange of images between peers. Certainly, a fair judgement by a professional wishing to apply this guidance to a peer-on-peer sexting incident might be, to begin with the Gravity score being 3 and, given the nature of the exchange of images (i.e. distribution) come to the conclusion that they should increase the gravity of the incident, and conclude that the young person should be charged.

There are no mitigating factors listed in the Gravity Matrix. Therefore, applying this process as directed by the guidance, the gravity of any charge related to section 1 of the Protection of Children Act 1978 can be no lower than 3 and there would be no situation where a community resolution (i.e. an Outcome 22) could be applied.

Take the scenario of two young people, aged 15, in a relationship and exchanging images consensually, with no suggestion that the images are shared further. One of the young people's parents might access the device (we have been told by many parents that they access their children's devices to "make sure they are safe") and see the images, and call the school. The school, mindful of the legalities of these scenarios, based on safeguarding training they received where the trainer simply stated that teen sexting is criminal under section 1 of the Protection of Children Act 1978, then call the police. The young people are spoken to and have phones confiscated, or searched in front of parents, school staff and police. Police refer to youth justice professionals who then make use of the out-of-court disposal guidance which directs them to the Gravity Matrix, and concludes that because the images apply under the act, and have been distributed, the gravity must (as defined in the guidance) be 4, and the young people should be charged. Whether this charging decision gets past Crown Prosecution Service public interest tests—as discussed in Sect. 4.1—remains to be seen (and in reality it is extremely unlikely they would) is mote—the young people who are doing nothing of harm, but viewed as illegal under a law developed to protect, rather than prosecute, young people, end up being charged based upon the guidance afforded to professionals who are unlikely to have received specific training on this aspect of digital practice.

5.3 An Analysis of Intervention at the Grass Roots

"Online abuse and its impacts flow into and beyond online platforms and require a contextualised understanding of technology and its role and function in the lives of users and societies" (Salter, 2017, p. 28). In bringing our empirical reflections to a close, we reflect in this section on discussions with both policing and youth justice practitioners that we meet during our work. We do this to triangulate the threads that permeate this text around the challenges of policing a behaviour that is both widespread and, for the majority of those engaging in it, harmless, against a legislative and policy backdrop centred on the application of out-of-date, inappropriate legislation because of adultist discomfort in young people having sexual agency. That is not to say that there are not some cases where there is undoubtedly a criminal element where the law should, and indeed has, be applied. For example, the case of the young man selling images of his ex-girlfriend discussed in Chapter 2 seems entirely appropriate.

Nevertheless, our work which has taken place over many years shows that in most cases, the law is problematic and applied disproportionately as a vehicle for prohibition, rather than pragmatically to support young people. While we commenced this work early in the twenty-first-century, policymakers still take a prohibitive view (an example of which will be explored in the following chapter) and the educational messages have not change. We have, from Chapters 2 to 4 explored how this impacts young people and we have presented considerable data on that "state of the nation". From this, we can see that:

1. Young people are still being charged for this "crimes"
2. The application of this legislation to teen sexting incidents is acknowledged as rarely passing a public interest test by the Crown Prosecution Service
3. The measures introduced by police and youth justice to try to mitigate aspects of criminality related to teen sexting are being applied, but not in a consistent manner
4. As a result of (3), outcomes for young people will remain inconsistent too.

Speaking to practitioners who are in the unenviable position of making decisions on how guidance to apply gives us an opportunity to reinforce our own views and help better understand the quantitative data presented in Chapter 4. During the development of this book, we have spoken to police professionals in three different forces and youth justice practitioners in three different local authorities. While ethical governance was, of course, in place for these discussions, we do not wish to divulge further detail as it was made clear to professionals that the conversations were confidential and non-attributable. Some of the professionals we had spoken to are still active in dealing with these issues on a day-to-day basis and while we believe nothing discussed places them in a poor light professionally, we are aware of the risks in challenging the status quo in child protection scenarios. However, we can state that in total we have, over the period this book was written, spoken with:

- 6 serving police officers with child protection and youth offending roles
- 2 former child protection police officers
- 4 youth justice practitioners
- 2 children's charity professionals with social work backgrounds and a history of dealing with youth online harms cases.

As stated above, we will not attribute comments to specific individuals. This is both to protect identities but also because the views of everyone we have spoken to were consistent—there we certainly no dissenters from the views expressed.

In detailing the discussions, we will explore the nature of the law and Outcome 21 and 22 interventions separately. While there are themes that cut across all these discussions it is worthwhile to discuss each individually.

One thing that was very clear from all our discussions with professionals was that they first thought the law was being applied in a manner for which it was never intended, and certainly not in a child-centric manner. They also stated that the guidance to which they are directed was generally not helpful and often contradictory. Professionals detailed a great deal of contradictory guidance, such as:

- CPS guidance on teen sexting
- ACPO Gravity Matrix
- Youth Justice Board Advice on Out-of-Court Disposal
- NPCC Outcome 21 guidance
- NPCC Outcome 22 guidance
- UKCIS guidance to school on sexting
- National curriculum for Relationships and Sex Education

The professionals all discussed how, while they knew that their profession would generally see teen sexting where it was consensual and not harmful as not something that required a criminal justice intervention, they felt that conflicting guidance and a lack of national policy (and political will to address the problems) meant that many colleagues would err on the side of caution (to reduce the professional risk in applying the guidance in a more pragmatic manner) and adopt conservative responses to disclosures. This is certainly something we have experienced in discussions similarly with education professionals over the years.

Some professionals we had spoken to had raised comparisons between the application of the law in offline sexual incidents and those with an online element, such as teen sexting. One professional in particular raised the application of Gillick competence and, more correctly, the Fraser guidelines (Wheeler, 2006) in supporting young people and making judgements on criminal thresholds. While Gillick competence is applied to the capacity of a young person to consent to receive medical advice and treatment while under 16 in the event that their parents might not consent and they might not wish their parents to know about the treatment—for example, the treatment of a sexually transmitted infection. The Fraser guidelines focus more on our area of interest, while following the same concept as Gillick—can a child under the age of 16 get advice and support around contraception and sexual health without parental consent or, to put it another way, can a professional support a minor below the age of consent in engaging in sexual acts, even though, legally speaking, what the child is doing is illegal?

The Fraser guidelines state that a professional should be satisfied with the following:

- *the young person cannot be persuaded to inform their parents or carers that they are seeking this advice or treatment (or to allow the practitioner to inform their parents or carers).*
- *the young person understands the advice being given.*
- *the young person's physical or mental health or both are likely to suffer unless they receive the advice or treatment.*
- *it is in the young person's best interests to receive the advice, treatment or both without their parents' or carers' consent.*
- *the young person is very likely to continue having sex with or without contraceptive treatment.*

One professional discussed a case where police were made aware of two fifteen year olds who were in a relationship and having consensual sex. While, by the letter of the law, these young people were below the age of consent and technically committing a criminal act, the application of Fraser guidelines to this case resulted in an acceptance that the young people were capable of consent and were not at risk. In this specific case, it was described that they were not "crimed", and there was no application of a crime outcome (for example OC22). Instead, it was recorded as a "Crime Related Incident". A Crime Related Incident (CRI) allows a police officer to record a crime but no details of the individuals involved. It is defined as not record of individuals. HM Inspectorate of Constabularies (2014) as:

> *a record of an incident reported to the police which would ordinarily amount to a notifiable crime, but is not recorded as a crime. This can happen for the following reasons: when the incident is reported by a third party (not on behalf of the victim) and the victim declines to confirm a crime occurred; where the victim cannot be traced; when the incident is being dealt with and recorded by another police force; or where the NCRS or HOCR direct that a crime should not be recorded (e.g. certain offences which occur in schools which are required to be dealt with by the school and not recorded by the police)*

It was the view of this particular police officer that while this is not an unusual practice for police to make use of a CRI for this sort of incident, they were not aware of its application to online sexual activities, perhaps because there is no guidance that supports it. Certainly, other police professionals we spoke to felt that this would be an appropriate response to consensual image exchange, they had not seen it being used in the context of teen sexting.

When this was explored further, particularly in the discussion why this might not be happening, there was a general view that the Outcome 21 direction had now made it "too easy" to be applied without the need for further justification. There would be no need to make a judgement call about competence, and the crime would be both recorded and closed with the use of an Outcome 21. It was acknowledged that an Outcome 21 would, arguably, be a worse outcome than a CRI, but it was simply easier to do within the guidance presented to the police.

As Hales (2018, p. 8) points out that "in considering the interaction of the law and police crime recording and counting practices, it is hopefully clear that it is difficult to understand the nature of 'sexting' offences from the kind of data published recently by the NPCC". Certainly, the use of Outcome 21 to end the case, and the recording of that case, we viewed as a reason why, in some of the quantitative data we have presented, Outcome 21 was used a great deal. As we were told by one officer, an investigation might take days to conduct and arrive at a decision to charge. Far better, upon visiting a school and a quick discussion with "offenders" in the heads office to all agree to put it down as an Outcome 21 and the young people are unlikely to hear about it again—the whole thing can be cleared up in a day and on the surface of things it would seem to be a better outcome for all.

While there was a great deal of empathy for professionals who made use of this approach, arguably as a result of many police not appreciating the full implications of recording an Outcome 21 against a young person's criminal record, it was clearly viewed as problematic and, we would argue, goes against the motivations for the development of the Outcome 21 approach. While the motivations for the approach were centred on better outcomes for the young people, it is not necessarily the case, illustrated if we look at the wording of the statement issues to young people and parents should an Outcome 21 be recorded, presented in Sect. 4.1.

Professionals were also concerned that the ease at which an incident can be shut down with an Outcome 21 would also reduce the likelihood of detection of more serious harm, such as coercion and peer-on-peer grooming. The focus of the guidance on the act, rather than the motivations, means that any officer called to an incident where an Outcome 21 is agreed by all stakeholders might miss coercive control or threats to produce imagery, as not investigation is carried out. While from a process perspective, and in most cases where image exchange is consensual, an Outcome 21 might be considered more effective than investigation and charge, it might risk failing a victim who is too scared to disclose abuse or coercion in a light touch discussion, especially if the educational messages they have received have made it clear what they did was wrong.

It was acknowledged that police are often unwilling to act with discretion because it can come back to haunt them in the future. There is a fear that, while they know the law is not fit for purpose, not applying it introduces a professional risk, should a complaint against the officer be made. It was also acknowledged that it would be very unlikely that a given officer would have received any training around these issues, so any interpretation of the law and guidance is down to the judgement and implicit biases of the officer, and there is a strong risk that crimes (that might, for example, fall under section 41 of the Sexual Offences Act 2003 [ibid.]) are missed. While there was a general view that Outcome 21 had at least reduced the number of young people being charged for consensual image sharing, it was not viewed as a good solution.

Attitudes toward Outcome 22 were similar, and those who had worked with Outcome 22 diversions were unsurprised with our Freedom of Information findings. It was generally the view that there was some awareness of Outcome 22 being applied to sexting incidents, the guidance that had recently been released clouded the picture further, with one practitioner stating they felt that the guidance said, "Don't use Outcome 22, use Outcome 21, that was designed for sexting incidents, however, if there were other (unspecified) factors, you could use it". Which would certainly also be our interpretation of the new guidance. Given that there is little guidance that explores the motivations and contexts in which image exchange occurs, with a focus almost entirely on the act itself, it is no surprise that some practitioners would apply Outcome 22. There was also widespread agreement that it would be extremely unlikely that a practitioner would have received any training around how and when to use diversion and educational interventions, with a general view that training does not exist because there is little national policy on consistent application.

When asked how interventions were designed, and what type of diversion (for example, education, counselling, social care, etc.) would be most appropriate, there was agreement that while there were tools available to help, most of the time it was done in an ad hoc manner. This was not necessarily viewed as always being a negative thing. By adopting an "ad hoc" approach, those who were perhaps working with the young person already (for example if they were under social care or had learning support in school) could be involved in the decision-making process and the intervention could be more personally tailored for the young person.

However, it was also acknowledged that the foundation of any intervention is the negotiation between practitioners in the youth justice system, so it might involve youth justice practitioners, social care, police and schools. While the stereotype of police wanting prosecutions and charging, and generally adopting a more "hardnosed" response to the incident was not borne out in our discussions (with many saying police officers would go out of their way to work with the best interests of the young person) it was acknowledged that "compromise" interventions were often the outcome from these discussions. Again, when asked whether any of the stakeholders in the decision-making process were likely to have received specific training around online harms, most felt this would be extremely unlikely.

We were told by one police officer that in a case with which they were involved, it was decided that the best outcome would be an educational intervention. There was a general feeling that the young person did not understand the issues around the risks in the exchange of images and further sharing, so they should be given the opportunity to learn. However, there was also a view that this was "giving them enough rope to hang themselves" such that if they were to engage in further image exchange post intervention, there would be less resistance to charging them because they "should know better" post intervention. When it was asked what the educational intervention was, we were told that the young person was given some videos from the Child Exploitation and Online Protection (CEOP) ThinkUKnow resources.[3] While there is nothing specifically wrong with the resources in the ThinkUKnow programme (indeed we work with many schools that use them effectively in education programmes), the delivery approach was not managed—the young person was simply told to watch the videos, and that was the end of the intervention. We asked if there was further follow-up with the young person to test the impact of the "learning". We were told no there was not.

While Outcome 22 might be considered a more progressive, youth-centric, response to child-on-child incidents, the potential for better

[3] See https://www.thinkuknow.co.uk/. Accessed January 2023.

invention has to centre on the efficacy of the intervention and also an evaluation of the impact of the intervention. It is not enough, surely, to simply tell a young person to watch some videos, there is a need to explore whether they have learned anything from them. It would seem, from our discussion, that interventions were rarely long term or involved much investment of resources. Sadly, this is not surprising given the lack of national support or investment in the criminal justice system over recent years. However, we would argue that the potential for an Outcome 22 intervention to divert a young person from a criminal path has to be dependent on the design of the intervention and the knowledge of the designers, and the measurement of the impact. And our discussions highlighted little rigorous evaluation or the use of evidence to show change. More it was put in place as "something", rather than the consistent, rigorous application of well-developed resources. Moreover, while in some cases a young person's school was involved in an intervention, this was not common practice, and educational interventions were developed by professionals with no training in education. While the Outcome 22 model does give the opportunity for multi-stakeholder input, time pressures often made it more likely that it would be designed quickly by a youth justice professional with little consultation with others. And we can hardly be surprised interventions are not evaluated as a result of workload pressures.

5.4 Facing the Policing Challenges

In closing out this chapter, which, compounded with the chapters that come before it might be entitled "What isn't working", we will progress on in the final chapter to a discussion on what a progressive policing approach to teen sexting might look like. However, we would reflect upon one key issue.

It is extremely unlikely that a more consistent, young person, best interests, focus will ever come into being without a change in the law. The view of those we interviewed was that there would be little to no resistance from any police about a change of law—there are very few police officers who feel that the law applied in this context is useful and helps them do their job effectively. There is general acceptance it's not fit for purpose and professionals engaging in daily struggles to achieve the best outcomes for young people while restricted by both the law and the complex and contradictory nature of guidance that has been developed to keep up with online behaviours.

Nevertheless, we have encountered professionals, both over the duration of the project that resulted in this book, and more generally in our many years working in the area of teen sexting, who know something needs to change. In the final chapter of this book, we draw some of these discussions, alongside our many conversations, together, to explore what a youth-centric, effective response to teen sexting might be, such that professionals can support true victims of harm while supporting those who might be engaged in these behaviours to understand the risks and how to mitigate them, without fear of prosecution for doing something that, if they were an adult, they would be protected in law. It is important that in addressing a more progressive future, it is not simply a case of changing the legislation. It needs the many stakeholders who have roles to play in supporting young people to understand their lives, to be informed by evidence and not our own biases, and to understand that prohibition will never be an effective solution. In fact, we would argue, hoping for a solution is the starting point for failure.

References

Hales, G. (2018). *A 'Sexting' surge or a conceptual muddle? The challenges of analogue law and ambiguous crime recording* (Perspectives on Policing Paper 4). The Police Federation. https://www.police-foundation.org.uk/2017/wp-content/uploads/2010/10/perspectives_on_policing_sexting_FINAL.pdf

HMIC. (2014). *Crime recording—Making the victim count.* https://www.justiceinspectorates.gov.uk/hmicfrs/wp-content/uploads/crime-recording-making-the-victim-count.pdf. Accessed January 2023.

Jackson, S., & Scott, S. (2004). Sexual antinomies in late modernity. *Sexualities, 7*(2), 233–284.

Prout, A. (2000). Children's participation: Control and self-realisation in British late modernity. *Children and Society, 14*, 304–335.

Salter, M. (2017). *Crime, justice and social media.* Routledge.

Taylor, M., Holland, G., & Quayle, E. (2001). Typology of pedophile picture collections. *The Police Journal, 74*(2), 97–107.

Wheeler, R. (2006). Gillick or Fraser? A plea for consistency over competence in children. *British Medical Journal, 332*(7545), 807.

Youth Justice Board. (2019). *How to use out of court disposals*. https://www.gov.uk/government/publications/how-to-use-out-of-court-disposals/how-to-use-out-of-court-disposals-section-1-case-management-guidance. Accessed January 2023.

Youth Justice Legal Centre. (n.d.). *ACPO Youth Gravity Matrix*. https://yjlc.uk/sites/default/files/ACPO%20Youth%20Gravity%20Matrix.pdf. Accessed January 2023.

CHAPTER 6

A Progressive Future?

Abstract Based upon evidence presented through many years of research, we argue that it is time to try something different and develop policing interventions that are mindful of children's rights and support, rather than criminalise victims. We further challenge professional biases and highlight the need for evidence-based responses and the failures of prohibitive social policy. Drawing upon another area of failed social policy, the notorious "war on drugs", we demonstrate how more success in this area has come as a result of evidence-informed policy and harm reduction approaches, which acknowledge the risks associated with social harm, and acknowledge an informed user is a safer one who can mitigate risk. We propose a harm reduction model for teen sexting and argue that a new approach is essential in order to break the cycle of prohibition and policy failure.

Keywords Teen sexting · Online safety bill · Digital natives · Professional bias · Harm reduction · Progressive policy · Evidence-based policing · Children's rights

A. Phippen and E. Bond, *Policing Teen Sexting*, Palgrave's Critical Policing Studies, https://doi.org/10.1007/978-3-031-31455-1_6

6.1 Teen Sexting as an Error of Judgement

Laura Ferris (Cons)[1]

As the Minister will know, sexting means the exchanging of intimate images by, typically, children, sometimes on a nominally consensual basis. Everything I have read about it seems to say, "Yes, prima facie this is an unlawful act, but no, we do not seek to criminalise children, because we recognise that they make errors of judgment." However, while I agree that it may be proportionate not to criminalise children for doing this, it remains the case that when an image is sent with the nominal consent of the child—it is nearly always a girl—it is often a product of duress, the image is often circulated much more widely than the recipient, and that often has devastating personal consequences for the young girl involved. All the main internet providers now have technology that can identify a nude image. It would be possible to require them to prevent nude images from being shared when, because of extended age-verification abilities, they know that the user is a child.

The above quote is taken from a recent political debate about the Online Safety Bill 2023, a proposal by the UK government to "make the UK the safest place to go online in the world" (UK Government, 2022). While much of the bill, and the subsequent debate looks more generally at online harms, this comment in particular gives us much to unpack on the policy position.

Firstly, the MP is acknowledging that the law is not fit for purpose but makes no call for it to be changed. Surely this would be a good opportunity to call for a change in the law so that it "prima facie" it is no longer an awful act. However, perhaps the next statement highlights why this was not the case, claiming any child exchanging images is making "an error of judgement", which seems to us to reflect the victim blaming mentality that has permeated attitudes towards teen sexting for many years. While there are certainly some risks in engaging in the exchange of intimate images, does this mean that anyone who engages in it, of whatever age, is making an error of judgement. Once against the onus of fault falls upon the sender of the images, not the person who decides to non-consensually share them. The MP then goes on to describe a worst-case scenario to

[1] Hansard. 12 May 2022. Volume 724. Column 110. https://hansard.parliament.uk/Commons/2022-12-05/debates/E155684B-DEB0-43B4-BC76-BF53FEE8086A/OnlineSafetyBill. Accessed January 2023.

illustrate her point, rather than acknowledging a great deal of intimate image exchange at any age takes place within respectful and consensual boundaries and the issue is not the act, but the discomfort with young people doing what is widely accepted among the adult population. That is not to say that we think young people should freely engage in the exchange of intimate images, just that we would rather those who are harmed are protected by policymakers, rather than being seen to have made an error of judgement.

However, perhaps the most problematic aspect of this statement is not the victim blaming, but the assumption that technology can solve this problem. Rather than call for a change in the law to support victims and bring the legislation in line with protections for adult victims of the non-consensual image, or calling for support for police in being able to achieve this within the restrictions of the failing legislation, she instead claims that service providers "have the technology" to detect and prevent the transmission of an intimate image by a minor. This is certainly not the only time a politician has claimed this (for example, see Phippen & Bond, 2020), and we are sure it will not be the last. However, as discussed in Phippen and Bond (2020), it is simply untrue and an exploration of the application of image recognition technology to detect intimate images of children results in inaccurate identification and training corpora that would demand private sector companies possess large volumes of intimate images of children for their algorithms to use.

It is little wonder that policing this issue is as problematic as it is, given the political discourse and the unwillingness, even when presented with an ideal opportunity, for policymakers to work toward progressive, victim-centric, legislation. And this, we would of course argue, is far more in line with what young people are calling for and most certainly more in line with evidence-based policing approaches, as illustrated by Knutsson and Thompson (2017):

> Given the credibility EBP is currently enjoying with both practitioners and government, it is timely to subject its underpinning logic to thoughtful scrutiny. This involves deliberating upon the meaning of evidence and what different models of knowledge accumulation and research methods have to offer in realising the aims of EBP. The communication and presentation of evidence to practitioner audiences are also important aspects of EBP, as are collaborative efforts to 'co- produce' new knowledge on police practice. (p. 1)

In updating our empirical work to the most recent aspects, the concept of co-production, and the need for multiple stakeholders, are brought into sharp focus.

6.2 Headstart Kernow

Headstart Kernow commenced in 2017[2] and continues at the time of writing. This project is a large local authority drive project that explores early intervention approaches to supporting children and young people with mental health issues. Within the wider project was an element regarding the impact of digital technologies on children's mental health. A decision taken early in the project was that there was insufficient literature and practice to draw conclusions regarding whether there was a causal link between mental health and different aspects of online behaviour, so we adopted a grounded approach that would form original views from young people themselves which would inform future project goals around how best to support professionals around different aspects of children's mental health practice.

Adopting a similar approach to other pieces of work, we used qualitative discussions to explore attitudes among young people, in both primary (aged 4–11) and secondary (aged 11–18) settings, and using a semi-structured approach involving workshops, discussion groups and interviews, spoke to over 1000 young people. While most of these discussions fall outside of the scope of this book, it was clear that there would not be seismic change from other pieces of work we had conducted more specifically around teen sexting. What was clear from our discussions was one of the core problems young people felt was a lack of concern by adult stakeholders in supporting them when online harms occurred. In something of a déjà vu experience, they disclosed that educational messages tended to be prohibitive and threatening (the now far too familiar "don't send nudes, it's illegal", "don't say anything offensive online, it's illegal", "don't look at pornography, it's illegal") and in the event of disclosure or even asking a question beyond the prohibitive mindset, the view was that, in general, responses would be negative at best and hysterical at worst. Far

[2] Phippen, A., & Street, L. (2022). *Digital resilience tool*. https://www.headstartkernow.org.uk/Digital/Headstart%20online%20resilience%20tool%20WebV2.pdf. Accessed December 2022.

better, they told us, to sort things out with your peers rather than involve adults in resolution.

These views were somewhat confirmed by discussions with the children's workforce (with conversation with teachers, police, social workers and safeguarding professionals within local authorities). Views were generally supportive of ethos but biases were writ large. Firstly, there was little distinction between different professions—views tended to share what we had already experienced in different pieces of research, prohibitive views were prevalent and there was a lot of deflection, with comments such as (unsurprisingly) "This sort of thing is normal to them", "We can't keep up with the technology they use" or the perennial favourite "They're the digital natives, they should know what they are doing".

The term has its roots in a much-cited article (Prensky, 2001), that separates the population into Digital Native and Digital Immigrants, their separation determined merely by birth year. The concept is a simple one and stands up to "gut feel"—people born into an era where they are exposed to digital technology at an early age are immediately comfortable with it. Those who adopt digital technology in adulthood do not have this innate ability. However, upon closer inspection, the very concept is somewhat ridiculous and there is little evidence to support it (Helsper & Eynon, 2010). Nevertheless, it remains part of the online safeguarding lexicon to date as it typically aligns with the prevailing value biases of individual experiences, especially when a term with such a zeitgeist perception makes one feel intellectual when delivering a line like:

> *"Well children these days are all digital natives, it comes naturally to them".*

We still experience this sort of statement far too often in child protection and safeguarding conferences. We would suggest that what the person delivering the statement means is either:

> *"They're digital natives, they should know about this sort of thing, and it's therefore their fault if they are harmed"*

Or:

> *"I'm not a digital native like they are, they know more than me, and therefore I shouldn't have to help them".*

However, perhaps the strongest piece of evidence that supports the views of the young people that it's best not to disclose to adults comes from a small vignette that formed part of the development of a resource aimed to support professionals in their decision-making post disclosure.

Using a similar model to the well-known Red/Amber/Green traffic light tools that professionals already used for consider harmful sexual behaviours (King-Hill, 2021), we developed a tool (Phippen & Street, 2022) that professionals might use to look up a disclosed online behaviour to determine whether or not they should be concerned about it, and whether the disclosure required further investigation. The motivation for this tool came directly from young people with whom we had spoken, and, as with most activities within the project, once the tool had been drafted, we worked with young people to refine the placement of behaviours based on age groups, and moved between behaviours that might be considered harmful, possibly harmful or not harmful. In total 155 behaviours were listed and would be listed against different age groups to show that, as young people mature, some behaviours that might be considered harmful at an early age would be less to worry about should they be older. For example, an issue such as voluntary accessing to pornography would always be considered harmful for primary-aged children became less harmful through teenage years.

Within these classifications were a few that related broadly to teen sexting, such as voluntarily sharing a requested image, being pressured into sharing, and the non-consensual sharing of nudes to others. In general, those that were not coerced, in teenage categories, were classified by young people we spoke to as "possibly harmful" and non-consensual or pressured acts to be "harmful". They had a typically mature view of these behaviours and pointed out, yet again, that sharing of intimate images is part of a lot of relationships and generally does not go further than the sender and recipient. However, they were clear that non-consensual sharing was unacceptable.

As part of the development of this tool, it was our intention to work with another charity that supports the children's workforce around sexual health and relationships education. However, as an interesting confirmation of the views of young people throughout the project, it became evident that there would be problems around issues of the exchange of intimate images.

The charity was sent a draft of the tool after refinement with young people. After a long delay, the charity returned the tool prior to a meeting having made some amendments. What was clear was that the amendments included moving all aspects of intimate image sharing to "Harmful", regarding aspects of consent. When challenged on the view that any sharing of intimate images has to be harmful, given that many young people do this without any harm, we were told it had to be harmful because it was illegal. Given the nature of the charity, we asked whether they would share a similar view should a young person under the age of sexual consent disclose that they were pregnant. "That's different" we were told because that was a sexual health issue. It would seem, in the view of professionals (with many years of experience around sexual health and relationships education) in the charity that online issues followed a different ethos to those offline. Or, perhaps, "we don't understand these issues, and don't agree with them, therefore lets hide behind the law".

The Headstart Kernow case study illustrates two things—firstly, young people are still saying that they are still receiving prohibitive messages as "education", and secondly that safeguarding stakeholders are still bringing their own biases and discomfort with young people's sexual agency to discussions about how best to support them.

However, in developing tools to modify the views of the children's workforce, rather than resources delivered directly to children, we started to see that the challenge was not the behaviour of the young people themselves, but the prohibitive approaches by those who claimed to have their best interests at heart. If young people were better informed and could develop in an environment that would support them should they make what the politician appallingly referred to as an "error of judgement", they are far more likely to disclose and receive the support they were seeking. Or, to consider it from another perspective, informed, supported young people are far more likely to have better outcomes than those told to not do something because it was illegal or if, as a result of what they did they experienced harm, were told it was their own fault and they could go to prison!

6.3 Harm Reduction and Online Harms

It would be better, we would suggest, to take a step back from the technology focus around online harms such as teen sexting, and look at previous legal failures where prohibitive approaches have been used to try to police social harms. We refer to the long "War on Drugs", and more specifically the Misuse of Drugs Act 1971 (UK Government, 1971).

While, arguably, drugs policy, at least internationally, has moved on from simple prohibition and the criminalisation of users, it has in its history a very clear "just say no" message. The parallels in debates between the introduction of the Misuse of Drugs Bill and the Online Safety Bill are interesting and certainly underscore the rhetorical devices used to argue for the need for these prohibitive legislations. In the introduction of the Misuse of Drugs Act, Mr William Deedes MP, stated:

> *This Bill is mainly about young children, or it should be, and the unnerving thing about this epidemic is the way, certainly in the United States, in which the age of infection creeps downwards.*
>
> *Differs because the MODA 1971 doesn't focus entirely on one stakeholder. However, the prohibitive nature of the legislation is directly comparable. These are both acts that intend to prevent a social "harm" from occurring – either the consumption and distribution of illegal drugs and the subsequent anti-social acts that occur as a result of drug consumption, or the consumption and distribution of harmful online content and prevention of abusive behaviours.* (Hansard, 1970a)[3]

In other words, drugs are harmful, and we need to protect society, especially children and young people. In the introduction of the Online Safety Bill, over forty years after the Misuse of Drugs Act, we can see very similar views:

> *For the first time, platforms will be required under law to protect children and young people from all sorts of harm, from the most abhorrent child abuse to cyber-bullying and pornography. Tech companies will be expected to use every possible tool to do so, including introducing age-assurance technologies, and they will face severe consequences if they fail in the most fundamental of requirements to protect children. The bottom line is that, by our passing this legislation, our youngest members of society will be far safer when logging on (Mrs Nadine Dorries).* (Hansard, 2022a)[4]

[3] Hansard. 25 March 1970. Volume 798. Column 1467. https://hansard.parliament.uk/Commons/1970-03-25/debates/f91449c8-2f64-4b79-9bfc-0aa5f0c72908/MisuseOfDrugsBill. Accessed January 2023.

[4] Hansard. 19 April 2022. Volume 712. Column 96. https://hansard.parliament.uk/commons/2022-04-19/debates/F88B42D3-BFC4-4612-B166-8D2C15FA3E4E/OnlineSafetyBill. Accessed January 2023.

In the Misuse of Drugs Bill debate, it was acknowledged that the evidence base was not sufficiently developed. However, it was crucial a prohibitive approach was used. Far better, it would seem to prevent use than understand risk and harm in more detail:

> *But, at least, while we in this generation are searching for the causes of drug taking, let us not be responsible for any weakening in our attempts to stamp out what is at present a dreadful scourge. We know too little, even about the so-called benign drugs, to take any risks. As for the rest, their immediate and visible consequences are too dreadful to behold (Mr James Callaghan).* (Hansard, 1970b)[5]

> *We do not know what the psychological long-term effects are. Until we know, we must make it clear to the young that we do not know and that we maintain prohibition (Mr William Deedes).* (Hansard, 1970c)[6]

And a similar viewpoint was articulated by the Secretary of State about online harms in 2022:

> *Remember: we have been debating these issues for years. They were the subject of one of my first meetings in this place in 2005. During that time, things have got worse, not better. If we choose the path of inaction, it will be on us to explain to our constituents why we did nothing to protect their children from preventable risks, such as grooming, pornography, suicide content or cyber-bullying. (Mrs Nadine Dorries).* (Hansard, 2022b)[7]

The history of the "war on drugs" clearly shows a similar prohibitive mindset that risks criminalising users and attempts to deliver simple messages about stopping harms occurring by preventing the act of drug taking.

[5] Hansard. 25 March 1970. Volume 798. Column 1460. https://hansard.parliament.uk/Commons/1970-03-25/debates/f91449c8-2f64-4b79-9bfc-0aa5f0c72908/MisuseOfDrugsBill. Accessed January 2023.

[6] Hansard. 25 March 1970. Volume 798. Column 1460. https://hansard.parliament.uk/Commons/1970-03-25/debates/f91449c8-2f64-4b79-9bfc-0aa5f0c72908/MisuseOfDrugsBill. Accessed January 2023.

[7] Hansard. 19 April 2022. Volume 712. Column 98. https://hansard.parliament.uk/commons/2022-04-19/debates/F88B42D3-BFC4-4612-B166-8D2C15FA3E4E/OnlineSafetyBill. Accessed January 2023.

In the introduction of the Online Safety Bill, we can see very similar views:

> *For the first time, platforms will be required under law to protect children and young people from all Sorts of harm, from the most abhorrent child abuse to cyber-bullying and pornography. Tech companies will be expected to use every possible tool to do so, including introducing age-assurance technologies, and they will face severe consequences if they fail in the most fundamental of requirements to protect children. The bottom line is that, by our passing this legislation, our youngest members of society will be far safer when logging on. (Mrs Nadine Dorries)*[8]

As can be seen from the timing of the introduction of the Misuse of Drug Act, these prohibitive approaches in drug policy have been around for far longer than prohibitive online harms policy. More recently, however, there has been a large consensus around the need to move aware from prohibitive approaches to understand the motivations of users, the multi-faceted nature of drug use and evidence-led policy categorising harms, leading to the Vienna Declaration (Wood et al., 2010).

In some democracies, we have seen far more progressive drugs policy that looks very different to these prohibitive views. For example, the decriminalisation of all drug use in Portugal (Greenwald, 2009), alongside centres where people can safely take drugs, has not led to what some predicted would be massive increases in drug use and overdose. The US, where some states have been even more progressive and built markets around the sale of some previously illegal drugs, has, similarly, not seen increases in addiction or antisocial behaviour (Pardo, 2014).

Broadly, these progressive drug policy concepts, and the resultant programmes of intervention that have resulted from these more rights and justice-based approaches, are referred to as harm reduction. *Harm reduction*, in the drugs policy and education world, refers to policies and approaches that aim to minimise not just health, but social and legal impacts of drug use, focussing on supporting users in an informed manner that allows them to make more positive choices and mitigate the risks associated with the taking of illicit drugs.

[8] Hansard. 19 April 2022. Volume 712. Column 103. https://hansard.parliament.uk/commons/2022-04-19/debates/F88B42D3-BFC4-4612-B166-8D2C15FA3E4E/OnlineSafetyBill.

Four basic assumptions central to harm reduction have been defined as (Marlatt, 1996):

(a) *harm reduction is a public health alternative to the moral/criminal and disease models of drug use and addiction;*
(b) *it recognizes abstinence as an ideal outcome but accepts alternatives that reduce harm;*
(c) *it has emerged primarily as a "bottom-up" approach based on addict advocacy, rather than a "top down" policy established by addiction professionals;*
(d) *it promotes low threshold access to services as an alternative to traditional high threshold approaches.*

And the Harm Reduction Coalition in the US, defines eight Principles of Harm Reduction (n.d.), that can be summarised as:

- Accept drug use as part of our world and we should work to minimise harmful effects rather than just condemn them.
- Understand that drug use is complex and multi-faceted and harms occur on a continuum
- Quality of life is more important than prohibition in successful intervention and policies
- Adopt a non-judgemental, non-coercive provision of services and resources to drug users and the communities in which they live.
- Users' voice should be a central part of the creation of programmes and policies designed to serve them
- The primary agent of a reduction in drug harms is from informed users
- Recognise the complex social factors that impact upon drug use and drug-related harm
- Does not minimise or ignore the real and tragic harm and danger that can be associated with drug use.

Clearly, there are differences between drug harms and online harms; online harms are frequently the result of actions of others upon an individual, rather than the choices made by the person themselves, and there is a more complex relationship between different behaviours that might not meet legal thresholds and how these might be tackled. However, the nature of harm reduction is far more closely aligned with what young people (as we have extensively discussed in this volume) have told us about tackling online harms:

- Effective, progressive education delivered by those who understand the subject
- Non-judgemental and supportive responses to disclosures and support to mitigate risk
- Policies and legislation that support victims rather than criminalising them
- Tools and responses from platforms which mean when they report something they can see what happens and they feel they have been listened to.

And while the approach may be somewhat untested in tackling online harms (although some elements of the online harms literature have called for multi- rather than single-stakeholder responses and progressive education for many years), it is at least thoroughly tested in another area of social harm. And harm reduction drugs policy is informed by an evidence base that says providing honest information about risks and how to mitigate those risks helps more people keep themselves safe than simple prevention approaches (Werch & Owen, 2002).

What is clear is that a harm reduction approach cannot take the current "just say no" perspective on online harms, or the problematic "the platforms should stop this" narrative. The adoption of a narrow prohibitive, or even dystopian, approach to risk which prevents children and young people from accessing specific content, engaging with specific platforms or performing certain acts online, which wrongly assumes they miraculously become "safe" is ultimately doomed to failure. In complimenting an approach that adopts harm reduction at its heart, allowing young people to understand the risks in being online and how to mitigate those, rather than simply being told "don't do it", we would propose a model that encourages stakeholders to look beyond platform liability as a solution to online safeguarding and realise it is not as simple as demanding something should cease, and instead requires interaction by a wide range of stakeholders.

We would argue that Bronfenbrenner's (1979) Ecology of Child Development is a well-established and widely used model that can be adapted for online safeguarding. Bronfenbrenner's seminal work applied both nature and nurture perspectives to a child's development stating that their own biology is central to their development, but interactions with other actors in their environment, such as family, community and society all play a part in the development and action in one of these actors will impact across the wider ecosystem of development. Therefore, we can conclude, in order to provide the most effective context for child development, we should not just look at the child, but its environment as well. We have developed the Bronfenbrenner model to consider the ecosystem around online safeguarding and shown it can be applicable to both child (Phippen & Bond, 2020) and adult online safeguarding (Bond & Phippen, 2022). A child-centric model is illustrated in Fig. 6.1.

By adopting an ecosystem approach for child online safety, we can see the need for a breadth of stakeholder responsibilities for healthy development and safeguarding, and the interdependencies between them. The child, at the centre, has their own individual characteristics, like age, gender, (dis)ability and previous experiences, which will influence both the child's development and how they interact with their immediate environments, both offline and online. These characteristics will also influence

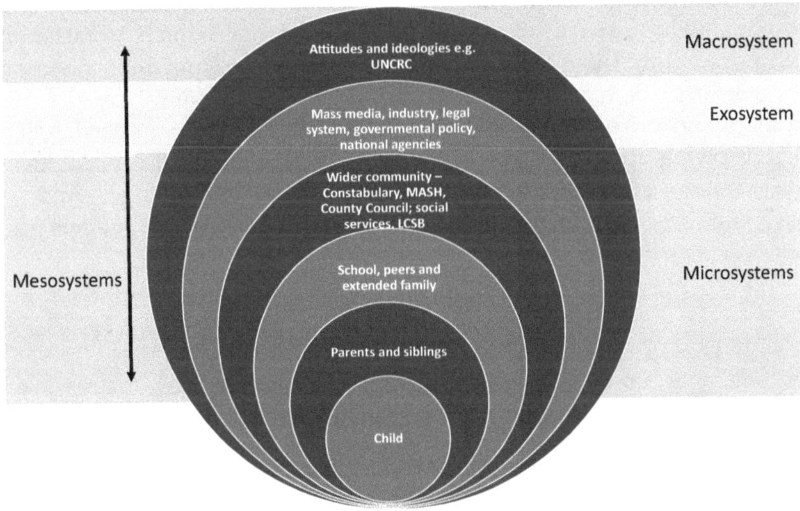

Fig. 6.1 An online safeguarding ecosystem

their vulnerability and resilience online. The microsystem, which refers to the institutions and groups that most immediately and directly impact the child's development, and how they interact with their immediate environments—both offline and online—will also impact on their everyday experiences and influence both their vulnerability and resilience.

The immediate spheres which influence a child's life and their landscapes of risk include their school teachers, peers, local law enforcement, social care and local authorities as well as everyday physical and virtual environments. All have statutory responsibilities for the welfare and safeguarding of the child both online and offline and, while industry does not sit within these microsystems, it exists in the broader exosystem that provides infrastructure for the child's online experiences and the views of other stakeholders within the microsystems.

The value of the model is that it shows the many different stakeholders in online safeguarding, and shows the importance of interactions (mesosystems) between them, as well as the distance a given stakeholder is from the student we wish to safeguard. Adopting a more holistic view of working with others to support young people in their online risk taking and decision-making is far more effective, as stakeholders can bring their own expertise to the safeguarding role.

Yet in a rush to claim platforms should eliminate harms and young people should "just say no", we are met with a domain which repeats itself and consistently fails young people. We need to do something different because what is very clear is things will not change until we do. We need to move from believing we can prevent harms to understanding that knowing about risk and reducing risk of harm are far more effective. We have evidence that this works in other social challenges. And we have considerable evidence that "just say no" or "errors of judgement" achieves very little.

6.4 What Works?

In reflecting upon what works, with a particular lens focussed on evidence-based policing and a harm reduction approach, we return to the model proposed above:

- Effective, progressive education delivered by those who understand the subject
- Non-judgemental and supportive responses to disclosures and support to mitigate risk
- Policies and legislation that support victims rather than criminalising them
- Tools and responses from platforms which mean when they report something they can see what happens and they feel they have been listened to.

Clearly, this is not something that can be achieved by a more progressive policing approach on its own, and nor should it be. As we have described above, safeguarding should pull in expertise across stakeholders, not pass the buck or expect someone else to do something. We would suggest that the main policing focus lies in non-judgemental and supportive responses to disclosures and support to mitigate risk, but we should also consider how tools and platforms might support progressive policing efforts.

We should stress that adopting a harm reduction approach does not mean starting from scratch, there is much that has already been discussed that certainly has a role to play, if used in a progressive and youth-centred way.

Outcome 21 is undoubtedly a more progressive response to teen sexting that arrest and charge. However, it does still present several problems, such as the association of the caution with the young person such that it will be retrieved in the result of a criminal records check. Furthermore, if it is used simply to bring any need to investigate to a halt, rather than being informed by an evidence-based decision that it is in the best interests of the young person, it might ultimately miss potential abuse or coercion between those being investigated in a sexting case. It is undoubtedly a far sight better than arrest and charge, but we would also propose that a Crime Related Incident record (as discussed in Chapter 5) might be a more effective use of policing mechanisms, due to the anonymity it grants.

Outcome 22 undoubtedly does have a progressive role to play if, again, it is applied within an evidence-based decision-making process. We would like to see clarification on guidance about its use in teen sexting incidents, as it is a very different intervention to Outcome 21. However, the guidance for application, and the associated tools (such as the Gravity Matrix) need serious revision if they are to be considered progressive and youth-centric. The consensual exchange of intimate images between two sixteen year olds should not be immediately graded at 3 with no opportunity for revision downwards.

Diversion and educational intervention have to potential to be extremely youth-centric and aligned with the specific needs of the young person. However, there is a need to develop diversions across the stakeholder space. In particular, it was clear from our discussions that education interventions can be designed on a somewhat ad hoc basis, with little consideration of the efficacy of the intervention. While there are resources such as the excellent So You Got Naked Online[9] and ProjectEVOLVE platform[10] that provide practitioners with a wealth of non-judgemental and age-specific learning support, they need to be applied within an effective intervention. Telling a young person to go and watch a video is not an educational intervention, it is clearing one's desk of a problem. Educational interventions should be designed with the involvement of education professionals, particularly those who have experience and training around the delivery of online safety.

And while we have been cynical about the role of technology in this domain, particularly with outlandish claims that phones could have software to understand if the user is under 18, detect the taking of an intimate image and prevent it from being sent. That remains a pipe dream that does not become closer to reality just because poorly informed politician claims it is possible.

Nevertheless, there is technology that can be used to support victims of non-consensual disclosure of intimate images that adopts a harm reduction approach that is both effective and gives agency to the victim.

The StopNCII platform[11] which is a joint project between Meta and the Revenge Porn Helpline in the UK, makes use of a technology called image hashing to allow a victim to provide platforms and service providers with a unique identifier for there images, without having to share actual images with the platforms. The technology that underpins the service is well established in child protection but for a different purpose.

[9] See https://swgfl.org.uk/resources/so-you-got-naked-online/. Accessed January 2023.

[10] See https://projectevolve.co.uk/. Accessed January 2023.

[11] See https://stopncii.org/?lang=en-gb. Accessed January 2023.

The Internet Watch Foundation[12] has proactive powers to search online for illegal images of children. Once images have been identified as child abuse or exploitation material the image will be processed using Microsoft's PhotoDNA algorithms,[13] which applies an algorithm to image data to produce a unique "fingerprint" for that image. For the IWF hash list, once the image has been identified and hashed using the Microsoft service, the hash will be stored. Therefore, a service provider can make use of the hashlist to process images it is accessing. It can then run the same PhotoDNA algorithm on any images it indexes, and if the hash matches, the platform knows, because it is in the IWF hash list, which means it has already been analysed by a human moderator and classified as illegal. Again, the "recognition" technology is very straightforward and easy to achieve—if the hash of the candidate image matches one in the hash list, it will be considered illegal and, at the least, blocked.

With the StopNCII approach, a victim of image-based abuse can apply the hashing technology on their own device, and then upload their hashes to the Revenge Porn Helpline service, which will then distribute them to service providers. Therefore if someone attempts to non-consensually share that image on a platform that uses the service, the posting will be blocked. Most powerfully, perhaps, is that the victim does not have to show their images to anyone, they are empowered to hash the images themselves and need share only the hashes.

This is a great example of stakeholder working together—technology that works is used by platforms, and a civil society service provides the contact point for victims. Until recently this service was, however, only available to adults. However, at the time of writing (January 2023), the National Centre for Missing and Exploited Children in the US (NCMEC) announced their Take It Down service,[14] which applies the same technology to a service for young people. In our view, this is the first service of its kind that tries to empower young people with technology, rather than simply telling them what they have done is wrong, and it is a fantastic

[12] See https://www.iwf.org.uk/. Accessed January 2023.

[13] See https://news.microsoft.com/2009/12/15/new-technology-fights-child-porn-by-tracking-its-photodna/#sm.0001mpmupctevct7pjn11vtwrw6xj. Accessed January 2023.

[14] See https://takeitdown.ncmec.org/. Accessed January 2023.

example of using technology within a harm reduction approach. There is no need for the young person to show the images to anyone, they simply hash them on their own device and upload them for platform partners to disseminate, and ensure any sharing results in a takedown.

6.5 A Change in the Law

As we have discussed above, harm reduction in the context of teen sexting has the potential to be a far more progressive and effective approach to policing teen sexting than those we have observed during the development of this project. It does, however, require stakeholders to work to their strengths for a common goal—the best outcome for any young person presented in the justice system. Nevertheless, we cannot bring this book to a close without returning to the fundamental problem—the law is being applied in a manner for which it was never developed, and there is political opposition to change existing legislation, even though there is widespread acknowledgement it is not working. One might imagine the resistance is due to the complexity required in changing the law. We feel this is a smokescreen and would propose, and put on public record, that a simple change needs to be made.

The new clause is a small modification to s1 of the Protection of Children Act under modification 1B:

> 1B Exception for criminal proceedings, investigations etc.
>
> ...
>
> (3) In proceedings for an offence under section 1(1)(a), 1(1)(b) or 1(1)(c) of making, distributing or possessing an indecent photograph of a child, the defendant is not guilty of the offence if he proves that:
> (a) He is under the age of 18, and
> (b) He is the sole subject in the photograph

This allows the removal of the threat of prosecution should an individual choose to self produce an intimate image and send it to a consensual recipient. However, it would still maintain legal recourse should a minor coerce another minor into a sexual act and produce an image.

6.6 Conclusions

In conclusion, sadly there is little in the analysis presented in this book that shows a progressive, child-centric approach to supporting those who become victims of image-based abuse. We are, we will stress again (as we have throughout this book), hugely sympathetic to those in the criminal justice system who are called upon to investigate and support those young people who attract the attention of the law as a result of safeguarding disclosures related to teen sexting. Or criticisms do not lie with those on the front line, but with those who have the power to change approaches and better support professionals working in this space. They need more support, better resources and more effective training. Clearly, in this book, we have shown that doing the same thing over and over again does nothing to change practice, and we realise we are moving into the second generation of young people who engage in these practices, and who are let down by those with a responsibility for their safeguarding, because the law does not work and no one is willing to change it.

However, we do see the potential for change, should those wish to engage with a more progressive approach, and we state in conclusion the need for policymakers to move away from moral panic and judgement of the upcoming generation and instead learn from the evidence base and authentic youth voice. They are very clear on what they would like and we have drawn upon our own work and that of other excellent scholars in an attempt to articulate this. Any progressive policy should:

- Adopt a harm reduction, education first approach to supporting young people around the risks in exchanging images, and honestly about outcomes should the law need to be applied
- Use the UN Convention on the Rights of the Child as the foundation for the development of any new legislation and policy around this area
- Support professionals working in safeguarding and youth justice with consistent resources, training and adequate time to be able to investigate and develop evidence-based interventions
- Develop legislation, as exists for adults, that punishes those who non-consensually share (should intent to harm be proven) and protect the victims of non-consensual sharing
- Speak to young people, listen, don't judge, and understand.

6.7 Personal Reflection

In bringing this book to a close, we will finish with a brief personal reflection. As presented in Chapter 2, with some extension in this chapter, we have worked in this area for many years. We have attempted to articulate the youth voice in this field for a long time, and young people have been telling us what they want since early in the century. Yet we still meet regularly with adult stakeholders who decide that they know best, ignore the evidence of the past and decide the best thing for young people is a good telling-off and a threat of prosecution. We would question how any adult who claims to have a passion for child safeguarding can come to this conclusion, but we still encounter these attitudes far too frequently.

We also meet stakeholders, including many police, who know that the approaches they have foisted upon them are not effective, and they want to do better. We hope the approaches described in this book help change the approach used to support young people in this area, but without national coordination and an appetite by policymakers to support young people rather than talking down to them, we are not sure they will. We keep on writing and we keep on presenting about what needs to change. And this is not simply our opinion, it is based upon conversations with thousands of young people and similar numbers of practitioners.

We note, just as we bring the writing of this book to a close, that another statutory body within the UK has produced yet another survey of young people, this time around the use of pornography (resulting in the shocking discovery that some young people access pornography at an early age, who knew!?), which calls on "someone" to do something. In this case, the Office of the Children's Commissioner has produced a report[15] whose core outcome is to "strengthen" the Online Safety Bill as a result of these findings. Interestingly, it does make mention of sexting related to self-produced pornography with this retrogressive statement:

> *Under the Protection of Children Act (1978)49 it is illegal to create or share indecent images of a child (even if the distributor is under 18) and the Sexual Offences Act (2003) criminalises 'sexual communication with a child'. It is worth noting that these laws were designed before the rise of social networking platforms and smartphones, and without recognition of the*

[15] See https://www.childrenscommissioner.gov.uk/report/a-lot-of-it-is-actually-just-abuse-young-people-and-pornography/. Accessed January 2023.

> *significant role they would come to play in sexual harassment and abuse, as well as in consenting teenage relationships.*
>
> *In 2016, the Home Office introduced 'Outcome 21' to allow police to respond in a proportionate way to youth-produced sexual imagery. However, the CCo have heard concerns from professionals about the use of Outcome 21 in practice and the potential, unintended, ways in which the Outcome may undermine safeguarding responses to peer-perpetrated intimate-image abuse.*

So once again a report coming to a similar conclusion that things aren't working, yet with little suggestion (from a body with the power to influence change) of how to improve outcomes for young people.

Having observed another policy report with "shocking" findings, can we make a call to stakeholders to please, stop doing surveys on the same things and coming to the same conclusions. Whether it is young people's use of pornography or their engagement with intimate image exchange, we know it happens. We don't need another survey that tells us this. How about, rather than being "shocked" we move the conversations on instead?

In their review of sexual harassment in schools in 2021 (OFSTED, 2021), the schools inspectorate for England, OFSTED, produced a research report which, somewhat unsurprisingly given the considerable evidence base, discovered such practices were prevalent. However, one piece of advice for school stands out:

> *In order to do this, they should assume that sexual harassment and online sexual abuse are happening in their setting, even when there are no specific reports, and put in place a whole-school approach to address them.*

Please can we adopt this approach across the safeguarding ecosystem, rather than stalling with claims of a need to "measure the problem first". What should the threshold for doing anything be? Surely one young person harmed as a result of the failures of the justice process is enough?

This brings us to the end of this work—should this be the last book we write on sexting? Perhaps in ten years time, we can return to this topic, and explore and measure the change that has occurred as a result of politicians setting policy that helps young people, and how a mainstreaming of harm reduction approaches are resulting in positive outcomes. However, we remain to be convinced that there is a willingness to change, as "just say no" is far easier than "what can we do to help?".

References

Bond, E., & Phippen, A. (2022). *Safeguarding adults online: Perspectives on rights to participation*. Bristol Policy Press.

Bronfenbrenner, U. (1979). *The ecology of human development*. Harvard University Press.

Greenwald, G. (2009). Drug decriminalization in Portugal: Lessons for creating fair and successful drug policies. Cato Institute Whitepaper Series.

Helsper, E. J., & Eynon, R. (2010). Digital natives: Where is the evidence? *British Educational Research Journal, 36*(3), 503–520.

King-Hill, S. (2021). Assessing sexual behaviours in children and young people: A realistic evaluation of the Brook Traffic Light Tool. *Child Abuse Review, 30*(1), 16–31.

Knutsson, J., & Thompson, L. (2017). Introduction. In J. Knutsson & L. Thompson (Eds.), *Advances and evidence-based policing* (pp. 1–9). Routledge.

Marlatt, G. A. (1996). Harm reduction: Come as you are. *Addictive Behaviours, 21*(6), 779–788.

OFSTED. (2021). *Review of sexual abuse in schools and colleges*. https://www.gov.uk/government/publications/review-of-sexual-abuse-in-schools-and-colleges/review-of-sexual-abuse-in-schools-and-colleges. Accessed January 2023.

Pardo, B. (2014). Cannabis policy reforms in the Americas: A comparative analysis of Colorado, Washington, and Uruguay. *International Journal of Drug Policy, 25*(4), 727–735.

Phippen, A., & Bond, E. (2020). Image recognition in child sexual exploitation material—Capabilities, ethics and rights. In H. Jahankhani, B. Akhgar, P. Cochrane, & M. Dastbaz (Eds.), *Policing in the era of AI and smart societies*. Springer.

Phippen, A., & Street, L. (2022). *Digital resilience tool*. https://www.headstartkernow.org.uk/Digital/Headstart%20online%20resilience%20tool%20WebV2.pdf. Accessed December 2022.

Prensky, M. (2001). Digital natives, digital immigrants part 2: Do they really think differently? *On the Horizon, 9*(6), 1–6. https://doi.org/10.1108/10748120110424843

UK Government. (1971). *Misuse of Drugs Act 1971*. https://www.legislation.gov.uk/ukpga/1971/38/contents/. Accessed January 2023.

UK Government. (2022). *World-leading measures to protect children from accessing pornography online*. https://www.gov.uk/government/news/world-leading-measures-to-protect-children-from-accessingpornography-online. Accessed January 2023.

Werch, C., & Owen, D. (2002). Latrogenic effects of alcohol and drug prevention programs. *Journal of Studies on Alcohol, 63*, 581–590. https://doi.org/10.15288/jsa.2002.63.581

Wood, E., Werb, D., Kazatchkine, M., Kerr, T., Hankins, C., Gorna, R., & Montaner, J. (2010). Vienna Declaration: A call for evidence-based drug policies. *The Lancet, 376*(9738), 310–312.

Index

A
adultist, 4, 19, 23, 25, 83
Aggravating Factors, 80
and uncontrolled distribution, 19
Article 12 (respect for the views of the child), 43
Article 13 (freedom of expression), 43
Article 16 (the right to privacy), 43
Article 19 (protection from violence, abuse and neglect), 44
Article 34 (sexual exploitation), 44
assembly(ies), 11, 15, 20, 27, 28, 30, 33, 34
Association of Chief Police Officers Gravity Matrix, 79

B
bias, 25

C
Child Exploitation and Online Protection (CEOP), 89
Childhood, 9, 18
Childhood sociology, 18
child pornography, 20, 45–47, 50, 51, 53, 61
children's rights, 11, 12, 18, 25, 42, 43
coercion, 2, 15, 19, 23, 24, 26, 28, 31, 32, 44, 49, 54, 72, 80, 87, 107
College of Policing, 2, 42, 62
Commonwealth Criminal Code, 45
consensual, 3, 15, 23, 31, 42, 43, 45, 60–62, 66, 85–88, 94, 95, 108, 110
consent, 4, 23, 31, 44, 45, 48, 50, 52, 54, 55, 61, 85, 86, 94, 99
COPINE scale, 81
Crime Related Incident (CRI), 86, 107
Criminal Code of Canada, 46
Criminal Justice and Courts Act 2015, 44, 61

A. Phippen and E. Bond, *Policing Teen Sexting*, Palgrave's Critical Policing Studies,
https://doi.org/10.1007/978-3-031-31455-1

criminal justice system, 4, 21, 32, 55, 60, 75, 78, 90, 111
Crown Prosecution Service, 42, 60–62, 82, 83

D
Data Protection Act 2018, 31, 43
Davies, Geraint, 55
determinist theories of technology, 18
dick pics, 24
Digital Immigrants, 97
Digital Native, 97
disclose, 11, 12, 22, 23, 27, 30, 35, 43, 44, 56, 63, 88, 98, 99
disclosure, 21, 32, 35, 43, 44, 49, 96, 98, 108
diversionary activity, 64, 65
Domestic Abuse Act 2021, 44
don't judge, 29, 111
drug prevention, 20
drugs harms, 35

E
Earl of LONGFORD, 53
ecology of child development, 32
education, 2, 11, 13, 15, 20, 27, 29, 42, 43, 64, 65, 78, 85, 88–90, 98, 99, 102, 104, 107, 108, 111
educational intervention, 89, 108
educator, 33
empirical work, 4, 25, 34, 96
enforcer, 33, 34
ethnography, 4
EU Directive 2011/93/EU, 61
Evidence-based policing (EBP), 2

F
Ferris Laura, 94
Fraser/Gillick Competence, 85
Fraser guidelines, 85, 86
freedom of expression, 31
Freedom of Information, 59, 66, 68, 88

G
Gillick competence, 20, 85
grass roots, 4
Gravity matrix, 82
grooming, 2, 62, 80, 87, 101

H
Harm Reduction, 99, 102, 103
hash, 109, 110
hashlist, 109
Headstart Kernow, 32, 96, 99
Hicks, Robert, 52

I
illegal, 12–14, 20, 21, 24–27, 29, 31, 33, 35, 46–48, 55, 63, 82, 85, 96, 99, 109, 112
illegal drugs, 20, 100, 102
image hashing, 108
innocence, 9, 77
Internet Watch Foundation, 109
intervention, 32, 43, 64, 65, 74, 78, 79, 85, 89, 90, 96, 102, 103, 107
intimate images, 2, 4, 10, 12, 14, 19–22, 24, 33, 42, 43, 45, 49, 50, 53, 72, 94, 95, 98, 99, 108

L
legislation, 4, 5, 8, 9, 11, 14, 20, 24–26, 29, 35, 41–56, 60–62, 66, 68, 78, 83, 91, 95, 100, 102, 104, 107, 110, 111
legitimised sexual harassment, 15
listen, 25, 29, 111

Lord ROBERTSON of OAKRIDGE, 53

M
Mary Whitehouse, 49
Ministry of Justice, 56, 59, 66
Misuse of Drugs Act 1971, 99
mobile phones, 17
modernity, 9, 16, 78

N
National Society for the Prevention of Cruelty to Children (NSPCC), 26
non-consensual, 15, 98
non-consensually shared, 23, 53
nudes, 12, 22–24, 29–31, 63, 96, 98

O
online communication, 19
online harms, 3, 20, 55, 80, 84, 89, 94, 96, 99, 101–104
Online Safety Bill 2023, 55, 94
Outcome 21, 4, 42, 59, 62–66, 68, 69, 72, 73, 78, 80, 85, 87, 88, 107, 113
Outcome 22, 63–66, 72, 73, 78, 82, 85, 88, 89, 107
Out of court disposal, 78

P
Paedophile Information Exchange (PIE), 50
participatory research methods, 12
police, 1–4, 8, 20, 21, 26, 28, 30–35, 42, 43, 46, 48, 49, 55, 59, 61–63, 65, 66, 70, 73, 77–79, 82–84, 86–90, 95, 97, 99, 112, 113
policing, 1–4, 9, 32, 34, 42, 47, 60, 62, 71, 83, 90, 95, 106, 107, 110
practitioners, 5, 9, 23, 25, 78, 82–84, 88, 89, 95, 108, 112
private, 10, 14, 16, 43, 44, 46, 47, 49, 50, 55, 56, 95
Prohibition, 28
Protection of Children Act 1978, 44, 47, 49, 60, 61, 66, 75, 80, 82
PSHE curriculum, 25
public, 1–4, 8–10, 16, 21, 29, 30, 33, 42, 49, 51–53, 61–64, 66, 68, 82, 83, 103, 110

Q
qualitative research, 11, 13

R
Relationships and Sex Education (RSE), 20, 78, 85
resolution, 28, 34, 62, 82, 97
Revenge Porn, 8, 42, 108, 109
revenge pornography, 29–31
Rev. Ian Paisley, 52
risk, 2, 3, 8, 9, 12, 16–19, 21, 27, 32, 33, 35, 42, 43, 49, 60, 70, 85, 86, 88, 93, 101, 104, 106, 107
risk anxiety, 8, 9
risk management, 19
Risk Society, 19
Rogers, George, 52

S
self-confidence, 18
self- esteem, 18
selfies, 23
self production, 47, 62
Serious Crime Act 2015, 48, 55

sexting, 2–4, 8, 11–16, 19, 21, 24, 26–28, 31, 33, 34, 42, 47, 56, 60–62, 82, 85, 87, 88, 94, 107, 112, 113
sexual beings, 22
sexuality, 4, 8–10, 22, 23, 77
Sexually Transmitted Infections (STIs), 27
Sexual Offences Act 2003 (SOA), 48, 61, 88
sexual self-identity, 3
sexual stories, 10
shame discourses, 27
sharing, 3, 8, 14, 19–27, 31, 43, 44, 47–49, 54, 56, 61, 62, 66, 72, 74, 88, 89, 98, 99, 110, 111
slut shaming, 28
social construction of risk, 8
social media, 3, 8, 9, 16, 18, 19, 26, 29, 30
social studies of childhood, 12, 13
spatial control, 21, 34
StopNCII, 108, 109
surveys, 10, 14, 29, 33, 113
survey work, 13, 29

T

teen sexting, 2, 4, 7, 9, 10, 13, 19, 20, 23, 33, 34, 41, 42, 46–48, 55, 63–65, 71, 72, 75, 78, 82, 83, 85, 87, 90, 91, 94, 96, 98, 99, 107, 110, 111
The Civic Government (Scotland) Act 1982, 42
The Marie Collins Foundation, 12
The South West Grid for Learning, 11
Townsend, Cyril D., 47, 50
transformation of intimacy, 16

U

UK Safer Internet Centre, 49
UN Convention on the Rights of the Child, 42, 49
under Directive 2011/93/EU, 46
utopian goal, 23

V

victim blaming, 25, 28, 94, 95
victimisation, 21, 34, 45
Viscount BARRINGTON, 54
vulnerability, 8, 9, 53, 106

W

Warman, Matt, 56
webcam, 17
western culture, 10

FSC
www.fsc.org
MIX
Papier | Fördert gute Waldnutzung
FSC® C083411

Kolibri 360 GmbH
Ferdinand-Jühlke-Straße 7
99095 Erfurt, Deutschland
produktsicherheit@kolibri360.de